Praise for *New Black Man*

"You won't find many scholars with Neal's deep and abiding knowledge of contemporary black popular culture, and you won't find any able to throw down such head-noddin' prose."
—Robin D. G. Kelley, author of *Freedom Dreams: The Black Radical Imagination*

"*New Black Man* is a bold, riveting work. It probes the contested spaces of what it means to be black and male and feminist. Bristling with an insurgent balance between being critically street and radically smart, Mark Anthony Neal opens a wider space for the arrival of a twenty-first century model of black masculinity. His book is required reading for anyone interested in reimagining gender and popular culture in America."
—Alexis De Veaux, author of *Warrior Poet: A Biography of Audre Lorde*

"Engaging, thoughtful, and soulful, this important book is part cultural criticism and part blueprint for a new version of black masculinity (without homophobia and misogyny). I, for one, welcome the arrival onto the scene of the 'new black man'."
—Dwight A. McBride, author of *Why I Hate Abercrombie & Fitch: Essays on Race and Sexuality*

"Read Mark Anthony Neal's *New Black Man*. Here, Neal redefines the 'burden' and expands the struggle for a society free of denigration and violence."
—Joy James, author of *Shadowboxing: Representations of Black Feminist Politics*

"Mark Anthony Neal has always been a daring scholar, but in this work he does pirouettes on a razor's edge, deliberately and deftly defying the keepers of the weary worn 'race man' trope and all its essentialist trappings."
—E. Patrick Johnson, author of *Appropriating Blackness: Performance and the Politics of Authenticity*

"Mark Anthony Neal's *New Black Man* is a fascinating exploration of an important scholar's acknowledgement of black feminism as a central mode of cultural investigation and a mode of humane existence."
—Michael Awkward, author of *Negoti̶a̶t̶i̶n̶g̶ ̶D̶i̶f̶f̶e̶r̶e̶n̶c̶e̶ ̶R̶a̶c̶e̶,̶ ̶G̶e̶n̶d̶e̶r̶,̶ and the Politics of Positionality*

NEW BLACK MAN

Mark Anthony Neal

Routledge
Taylor & Francis Group
New York London

Routledge is an imprint of the
Taylor & Francis Group, an informa business

Published in 2006 by
Routledge
Taylor & Francis Group
270 Madison Avenue
New York, NY 10016

Published in Great Britain by
Routledge
Taylor & Francis Group
2 Park Square
Milton Park, Abingdon
Oxon OX14 4RN

Printed in the United States of America on acid-free paper
10 9 8 7 6 5 4 3 2 1

International Standard Book Number-10: 0-415-97991-9 (Softcover)
International Standard Book Number-13: 978-0-415-97991-7 (Softcover)
Library of Congress Card Number 2005005959

Library of Congress Cataloging-in-Publication Data

Neal, Mark Anthony.
　　New Black man / Mark Anthony Neal.— 1st ed.
　　　　p. cm.
　　Includes bibliographical references and index.
　　ISBN 0-415-97991-9 (pbk.) ISBN 0-415-97109-8 (hbk.)
　　1. African American men. I. Title.
E185.86.N395　2005
305.38'896073—dc22
　　　　　　　　　　　　　　　　　　　　　　　　　　　　　　　　2005005959

Taylor & Francis Group
is the Academic Division of Informa plc.

Visit the Taylor & Francis Web site at
http://www.taylorandfrancis.com

and the Routledge Web site at
http://www.routledge-ny.com

Dedicated to

Gloria Taylor-Neal, Misha Gabrielle Neal (Ya-Ya),
and Camille Monet Neal (Millie) and
Arthur Cleveland Neal, Jr. and Elsie Eleanor Neal
and "Mama Soul"—Dr. Masani Alexis DeVeaux

In Memory of Those Who Helped Me
Walk This Path

Bayard Rustin, Audre Lorde, Ella Jo Baker, June Jordan,
Nina Simone, Jason "Jam Master Jay" Mizell,
Laura Nyro, Donny Hathaway

I am a man of my times, but the times don't know it yet!

Erik Todd Dellums as Bayard Rustin in *Boycott*

My life is all I have/My rhymes, my pen, my pad/And I done made it through the struggle don't judge/What you say now, won't budge me.

Pharoahe Monch, "The Life"

Contents

Preface

So as usual you gonna make me write you a letter. I guess it's one of the rhythms of our relationship—you become closer to me in your remoteness, though I fully understand your distance this time around. I am truly sorry to hear about your partner's health. I know that it's weighing heavily on you and know that she—you—are in my prayers. I hope that B-lo is otherwise OK and that there are many women *and* men benefiting from your stewardship of the department. You don't need to hear this from me, but nevertheless I am so proud of you for accepting the challenge to build something that is so institutionally vital to not only the community in B-Lo but for all those still learning from your example from afar.

I could tell you about life in Texas, the brown-skinned woman and two brown-skinned little girls who all conspire to make mine a life worth living and a life well lived—I could tell you about a possible move in the fall, but that will wait for another time. This letter is about you—and me—but really you.

It was two years ago when you encouraged me to write from my heart about the black masculinity that I wear. "New-BlackMan" you called me and indeed it is a badge of honor even during those times when I feel I can't live up to its ideals.

As a tribute to you, this book would forever be known as *New Black Man*. Indeed this project has been a part of my life for two years, but truth be told though, when the contract was signed and the due date was set, I wasn't sure if I had the heart to do this.

It was during this time in the early autumn, when I was doing everything but *New Black Man*, that the galley for *Warrior Poet* showed up in the mail, all unannounced. I spent every free moment of the next week with *Warrior Poet*, obviously getting a privileged and intimate view of the woman who was Audre Lorde, but it was also clear to me that reading your words about her life gave me a closer glimpse into the *you* that you be. You have shared very little about yourself to me and after those quiet moments with *Warrior Poet* many of my unasked questions were answered. It was as if suddenly I realized that I was part of a lineage of women—Lorde, June Jordan, Toni Cade Bambara, Barbara Christian, Claudia Tate, Pat Parker, Beverly Guy-Sheftall, bell hooks, Michele Wallace, Joy James, Patricia Hill-Collins, Jewelle Gomez, Sharon Patricia-Holland, and of course You—and it was that lineage that demanded that I write this book. *New Black Man* has been a singular focus since that time and damn if it hasn't been a trip back to the *when* that I began to become the *me* that I be.

I don't know if you remember the first day I walked into your class—in a basement somewhere on the old campus— a class on "Black and Red" feminism. Only male in the room and I was five minutes late at that. And you never treated my presence in your class, among those women-thinkers, as anything exceptional. No, it was a chance to speak across the so-called divide. Paula Gunn Allen, Jewelle Gomez—just two of the women that I read that fall semester. Never thought a full decade later, I would look back at those days as the foundations of the man, the scholar, the thinker, the feminist that I think myself to be today.

Still remember another class—another room full of women like Anne Borden and our dearly departed Wanda Edwards, who in a quiet moment of self-doubt, willed me into the world that I inhabit today as an intellectual. Reading work by Stanlie James, Abena Abusia, Patricia Hill Collins. Not yet your son, but definitely *your* pupil—the one you would claim and who would never forget to claim *you*. I can remember meeting Joy James four years ago, right after I had reviewed her book *Shadow Boxing* as she wondered how "a brother like you" (meaning me) could give such an informed view of her work and when I mentioned your name and it was made all clear to her. Or when I sat in a bar in the ATL as these decidedly stylish and mature black women (Beverly Guy-Sheftall and Ayoka Chinzera) kept me out till all hours of the night (I couldn't hang) and wondered how I came to be the "NewBlackMan" that I still hope to be and when I mentioned your name they responded, "Oh, well you're family then."

This book has forced me to go back to my "birth" and in that regard your role as "Mama Soul" has never resonated so powerfully. Still got a deadline to hit, but I am in the best writing groove of my career, no doubt because of the inspirational forces that have conspired to bring me to this point in my life. There's so much else to talk about, like getting *us* on tape for four or five hours so that we can lay down the rhythms that I think could inform the futures of our respective disciplines and just simply finding out when we can both catch our breath and find out, truly, where we be in the world at the moment.

For now, I'm listening to Meshell Ndegeocello's version of Jimi Hendrix's "May This Be Love" which segues into Maxwell's version of Kate Bush's "A Woman's Work"—men and women speaking to and through each other from so many different vantage points—and this seems a fitting moment to bid adieu.

Love always,
Your Soul Baby

Acknowledgments

Masani—there really are no words. Ms. Gloria Taylor-Neal: "So what's your name, girl?"—and that's how we began back in the spring of 1982, riding on the uptown D-train. Twenty-three years later we have fourteen years of marriage and two daughters who keep us alive and vibrant. Though the grind and my ambition often keep me from saying so, I just wanted to let you know you're *still* the love of my life. To my "whurl-a-girls" and future Spelman women, Misha Gabrielle and Camille Monet, Daddy loves you so much and I owe you both for the life I now lead. Many thanks to the women who keep me grounded, challenged, and hopeful: Nic J, Ms. Faith Corbett (baby gurl, baby gurl!), Jeanette McVicker, Ms. Jiann Calhoun-Tate, Ms. Sonja Cherry-Paul, and Ms. Pamela Haith.

Many thanks to those fabulously brilliant "womens" who inspire me to be the best thinker I can be: Lisa "L-Boogie" Thompson, Sharon Patricia Holland, Joan Morgan (my very first sister-girl homie), Jennifer Devere Brody, Debra Dickerson (shout out to the Negro Breakfast Club), Daphne Brooks, Cynthia Fuchs, Janell Hobson, Esther Iverem (SeeingBlack.com), Habiba Ibrahim, Kim Pearson, Bianca Robinson, and Jennifer Williams. Brother pounds, "all-the-way 'round" for the *NewBlackMen* in my life: "Big Bruh" Dr. Julius Adams, Franklin Louis Paul, Jr., Sebastian Tate, Richard "The R" Iton, S. Craig Watkins, Nicholas Young (damn I miss those head-noddin', key-tappin' mornings at the 'Bucks), Wesley Taylor, Michael Eric Dyson, Jabari Asim, Kevin Powell, Christopher Johnson, and Jason Smith.

"I put hands my heart/That means I feel 'ya/Real recognize real and you lookin' familiar"—just a quick holler to those folk doing it for real in the field: Robin D. G. Kelley, Farah Jasmine Griffin, John L. Jackson, Jr., Todd "the Notorious Ph.D." Boyd, E. Patrick Johnson, Dwight McBride, Wahneema Lubiano, Maurice Wallace, Nichole Fleetweed, Ingrid Banks, Murray Forman, Guy Ramsey (Professor Funk), Valerie Smith, Noliwe Rooks, Lawrence Jackson, David Ikard, Craig Werner, Edmund Gordon, Jr., Michael Awkward, Joni Jones, Greg Dimitriadis, Marc L. Hill, Oliver Wang, Marcia Dyson, Yvonne Bynoe, Norman Kelley, Aldon Nielsen, Bahati Kuumba, Davarian Baldwin, Reiland Rebaka, William Jelani Cobb, Jeff Chang, Felicia Pride. and of course my new fam at Duke including Bayo Holsey, Charles Payne, Lee Baker, Houston Baker, Jr., Charlie Piot, Karla F. C. Holloway, and Thavolia Glymph. "Holla back, it's ya boy!"—thanks to Routledge's Bill Germano for his initial faith in a "100 percent intelligent black child" and my editor Matt Byrnie for always understanding a brotha's vision. Special shout out to Eric Zinner who really helped me focus in on what this book was about.

Many thanks to the folks who keep my voice up on the Web on a regular basis: Ken Gibbs and Kate Tuttle (Africana.com) and Sarah Zupko (Popmatters.com). And thanks to my students (past and present): Greg Carter, Holly Alloway, Terri McBrewer, Sanjay Mitchell, Zoe Bogan (Fredonia up in the house!), Brian LeMaster, Mark Cunningham, Maisha Akbar, and Kwame Baird.

To Mommy and Daddy, baby-boy getting his "Grown Man" on now, but always remember that them days at 1231 Fulton Avenue and 2802 Schley Avenue (in the "Boogie-Down" of course) were some of the best times of my life.

Introduction

walking like a natural man

This book was born thirteen years ago, when I walked into the home of legendary ethnomusicologist Charlie Keil and extended my hand for the first time to Dr. Masani Alexis DeVeaux. It was at a gathering of new graduate students in the American Studies Department at the State University of New York at Buffalo. By the end of that evening I had decided that this woman—not much taller than my own mother (4'11")—would be the person, the woman, to shepherd me through my pursuit of a doctorate. Alexis would join a list of women—the former Ms. Miller, Ms. Goodine, Ms. Riley, Mrs. Phipps, and Mrs. Karr—who were the only black teachers I had the privilege to learn with in over twenty years of formal schooling. And shepherd me she did. Three years after our initial meeting, I stood onstage as she draped me with the coveted hood that acknowledged my transition from doctoral candidate to Doctor of Philosophy (Ph.D.). But that was where our relationship really began. It would be another five years before I would see Alexis face to face again, but through a regular exchange of letters and far-too-few phone calls, we began to cultivate the relationship between "Mama Soul" and her intellectual son. Back in 1989, members of the hip-hop collective Native Tongues sang about how "Mama gave birth to the soul children." And indeed this "Mama Soul" did give birth to a soul baby, one who thought himself feminist and anti-homophobic.

Alexis and I rarely talked about *her* life. So many of our personal interactions when I was still at the University of Buffalo were framed by the seventy or so other students who also needed her time, and by her biography of Audre Lorde that would take her away from me for long periods of time. Thus those letters and phone calls took on a deeper significance, particularly when I began my career as a professor at the State University of New York at Albany. They became the space where we could be "mother" and "son." When Alexis and I did see each other again in early 2001, it was at the Progressive Black Masculinities Conference sponsored by the Baldy Center for Law and Social Policy at the University of Buffalo. I was only there because Alexis told the organizers that I should be there. Ironically, although I always understood a significant aspect of my work as being feminist, I had rarely given any thought to black masculinity. But as I sat there quietly listening to the other scholars assembled, including Alexis, Patricia Hill-Collins, Karla F.C. Holloway, Beverly Guy-Sheftall, Kendall Thomas, Michael Kimmel, and Athena Mutua, I felt both overwhelmed by the brilliance of their thinking and the feeling that somehow my work was out of place in this setting. The reality is that I had rarely written or talked about black men in the context of their masculinity—in the context of race, yes, but not as gendered beings. Yet Alexis seemed to understand that it wasn't about the texts I had written, but the text that I *was*. In other words, "Mama Soul" understood that her "Soul Baby" was a metaphor for the very progressive black masculinity that I thought I didn't have a grasp of. For Alexis, that metaphor was best represented in the term "NewBlackMan," the name she began to call me in her letters. I would like to think that she never thought of me, per se, as that "NewBlackMan"—I am certainly not deserving—but as a way to suggest that I embodied the possibilities of a black feminist manhood.

Shortly after the Progressive Black Masculinities Conference, I started writing a series of personal essays for the fledgling online magazine Africana.com. My first piece was a sweet remembrance of playing baseball as a child, but with the second essay something very powerful was unlocked. In that essay I talked about how vulnerable I felt after adopting my oldest daughter Misha Gabrielle (now six), and how this precious little brown girl with the feisty spirit had managed to save my life after years of struggling with a spiritually and physically debilitating bout with sleep apnea. I revealed how fatherhood had forced me to re-examine my thoughts about masculinity. After reading my essay, Alexis encouraged me to write a book about my experiences as a new father. In the aftermath of my getting treatment for my sleep apnea I witnessed an explosion of creative energy. My then-two-year-old daughter—my backseat interlocutor on everything from music to clothing styles to literary theory—was a critical component of those energies and I really wanted to talk about how fatherhood had literally changed my life in so many wonderful and poignant ways.

But as 2001 progressed, the 9/11 attacks and my own mortality came to dominate my thoughts. Having lived in upstate New York for most of the last decade, I had become familiar with the seasonal depression that came into my life as the autumn months got darker and colder. But 2001 was different. Like most Americans, the attacks on September 11th simply floored me. In my mid-thirties at the time, I had rarely given much thought to my own mortality. What happened on that day brought me face to face with the fleeting nature of our lives and the inevitability of my own demise. I really wasn't concerned much for myself, but was paralyzed at the thought that a premature death would leave my then-three-year-old daughter fatherless. For much of the next year after the attacks, I literally lived every day as if it were my last. And it was in that state of mind that I tried to create "living moments" for my daughter Misha, so that she could always remember them in the event that I wouldn't be around. Every night I tossed and turned in my bed, crushed by the look that I imagined would be on my daughter's face when she found out her daddy wasn't ever coming back. My wife is still wondering what was up when we hopped into the car during Thanksgiving weekend of that year and drove two hours into Vermont to visit Christmas Town, a year-round outdoor theme park. In my mind, it was a way to give Misha a "Christmas" in case I wasn't actually around for the real Christmas that was only a month away. As usual, I shared very little of these fears with anyone, including my wife, and dealt with my psychosis on my own, self-medicating with the music of Donny Hathaway and Laura Nyro.

The death of my father-in-law in early November of 2001 of a sudden stroke only intensified my fear of death. Willie B. Taylor's death made my fears very real and personal, as I tried to comfort my grieving wife and the two of us tried to protect Misha from the immediacy of losing her "Papa." At the same time I began to suffer from chest pains and considering my 250-plus pound frame, my fear of leaving this earth became very tangible in my everyday experiences. Even my first EKG didn't convince me that I was just tripping as my doctor looked at me incredulously when I told him my fears. Without a history of heart disease in my family, relatively decent cholesterol levels, a normal blood pressure, and none of the signs that suggest impending heart failure, I suppose my doctor thought I was just crazy. Upon further examination we found out the real culprit—acid reflux—largely brought on by too many fried foods and my habit of drinking up to eight cups of coffee a day. As the calendar turned to a new year, I made the decision, like millions of others, to turn to a healthier lifestyle: caffeine, dairy, and red meat were the initial things I gave up. By mid-2002, I had lost twenty pounds and dropped my cholesterol level forty points. I was perhaps coming to terms with the reality of my impending middle age. I wasn't crazy, but living with the emotions that so many who are responsible for children and family have to deal with. Then BJ Moore, one of my childhood friends, died suddenly of heart disease. Unlike my father-in-law, who had lived a full and fulfilling life in his seventy-two years, BJ was only thirty-three. Two years later I'm still grappling with BJ's premature death—he comes to me regularly in dreams—likely the product of some of the guilt that I felt for not keeping in touch with him in recent years.

One of the first things I did after hearing about BJ's death was to begin a morning walking regimen. Ostensibly an attempt to follow up on the healthy gains I made through diet, those early mornings with just the music on my portable CD player became the space where I finally came to terms with my own mortality. It was during one of those morning walks that *New Black Man*, the book, was finally birthed. One of my favorite discs during those early morning walks was Aretha Franklin's live recording *Amazing Grace* (1972), a recording that I had been listening to regularly for thirty years (it is one of my mother's favorites) and never failed to be moved by. And I was experiencing the sheer joy of Aretha's music and the sensuous energy that comes from a body in motion, when something profound clicked while listening to her version of the old Caravan classic "Mary Don't You Weep." There is a moment midway through the song where Aretha, the Southern California Community Choir, and the congregation are in such a rhythmic flow that it's impossible not to get caught up in the tight frenzy. I say "tight frenzy" because despite the general feeling of improvisational looseness, Ms. Aretha is quite deliberate in her delivery as she is, after all, telling a story. The story is of course that of a dead Lazarus and his sisters Mary and Martha, who after sharing their grief with Jesus are given the comforting words, "Oh Mary don't you weep, Tell Martha not to moan." The critical moment in the story and the song—the spiritual tipping point if you will—comes when Jesus decides to raise Lazarus from the dead. The moment gets retold in Ms. Aretha's singular fashion: "For the benefit of you who don't believe, who don't believe in me this evening, I'm gonna call him three times (Oh yes I am! Oh yes I am!)." And then Ms. Aretha utters that name three times. "He said *'Lazarus'* (call it now) ummmmm, *'Lazarus'*, hear my, hear my voice *'LAZARUS'*(!!!). . . . He got up walking like a natural man (oh, yes he did, oh yes he did)."

I've heard Aretha call Lazarus's name three times for thirty years, but that moment in the song had never resonated with me before as it did that July morning in 2002. In the words of Samuel L. Jackson's character from *Pulp Fiction* "I had what alcoholics refer to as a moment of clarity." Via the voice of Ms. Aretha Franklin, the story of Jesus raising Lazarus from the dead became a metaphor for how I viewed my own masculinity. The "little deaths" that I died (often as long as a minute) while suffering for a decade from sleep apnea as well as the "death" of how I viewed black masculinity before the adoption of my oldest daughter, were the foundations for a "rebirth," a raising from the dead, in which the voices of women such as Ms. Aretha, Alexis, the late June Jordan, and my colleague and friend Sharon Patricia Holland, whose book *Raising the Dead* unlocked formerly dormant intellectual sensibilities in my scholarly work, were absolutely critical.

It is crucial that readers understand that I am not the *New Black Man*, but rather that *New Black Man* is a metaphor for an imagined life, one that I fail to live up to every day of my life. *New Black Man* represents my efforts to create new tropes of black masculinity that challenge the most negative stereotypes associated with black masculinity, but more importantly, counter stringently sanitized images of black masculinity, largely created by blacks themselves in response to racist depictions of black men. The theme of the book is perfectly captured in a phrase from the HBO film *Boycott*, where Bayard Rustin (portrayed by Erik Todd Dellums) utters, "I am a man of my times, but the times don't know it yet!" *New Black Man* posits, indeed celebrates, new visions of black masculinity not beholden to conservative and essentialist notions of how black men should act in American society, a black masculinity that, for example, takes lessons from the progressive politics of the black feminist movement.

Source:
Neal, M. A 2006.
New Black Man.
NY: Routledge.

Chapter 1

there's a new black man
in america today

Author: MARK ANTHONY Neal

The Black Man is in crisis. And thus the theme of hundreds
of newspaper, magazine and journal articles, and conferences
over the last twenty years. This theme was perhaps best articulated in the article, "Who Will Help the Black Man?" the
cover feature in the December 4, 1994 edition of *The New
York Times Magazine*. The article featured a cross-generational
roundtable discussion moderated by journalist Bob Herbert,
who was joined by several prominent black men including then
National Urban League President Hugh Price, talk-show host
Ken Hamblin, filmmaker John Singleton, and scholar William
Julius Wilson, who penned the hugely influential books *The
Declining Significance of Race* (1980) and *The Truly Disadvan-
taged: The Inner City, the Underclass and Public Policy* (1987).
Herbert sets the tone of the discussion in his introduction
where he suggests that the "plight of the black men in the

1

nation's inner cities has been widely reported" but adds that it is the crisis of the black male underclass that "remains the pre-occupation of many Americans, none more so than successful black men in America."[1] And on cue, much of the discussion focused on the disaffected and demonized hip-hop genera-tion that we've all come to know quite well via MTV, Black Entertainment Television (BET), ESPN, Fox News, and daily newspapers such as the *Washington Post* and the *Los Angeles Times*. Though the roundtable discussants disagreed often about responses to the crisis of the hip-hop thug and his various incarnations and even disagreed to the extent that such figures should be viewed with scorn or sympathy, no one captured America's sense of young black men better than Ken Hamblin's quip that they were "black trash . . . people who prey on us and then turn around and encourage us to sit here as intellectual wizards, film makers, columnists, talk show hosts, members of black organizations and talk about what whitey did to us."[2]

"Who Will Help the Black Man?" was published at a moment when bookshelves were overrun with autobiographies by "suc-cessful" black men, all seemingly part of a veritable cottage industry of black man uplift literature, where black men from poor, deprived, dysfunctional, and single-parented backgrounds described their transition to well-adjusted, productive, upper-middle-class lives. This sudden hunger for black uplift litera-ture by both black and white audiences seemed to mark the change from the "dire" Reagan–Bush years to the Clinton "Big Willie" era and thus many of these tomes helped obscure the reality that the lowest economic tier was continuing to catch hell, despite the presence of high-profile black men like Colin Powell, Bill Cosby, Michael Jordan, Jesse Jackson, and Kenneth Chenault, to name just a few. Thus books such as Nathan McCall's *Makes Me Wanna Holler* and Brent Staples's *Parallel Time* were on everyone's must-read list and America felt good that the civil rights movement had succeeded and there might be a black president in the near future and no one was uncomfortable with the fact that a 6-foot-6 bald-headed black man with a basketball in his hands came into their living rooms on the daily to sell hamburgers, electrolyte beverages, and batteries.

In this environment it was perhaps easy to isolate the Tupac Shakurs, Allen Iversons, "Pookies," and Nushawn Williamses of the world and make them the reason why the black man has failed. They are "criminals"—trash—who listened to and made violent music, defiled black women, smoked crack, made fun of homosexuals, and had unprotected sex with minors. Hell, even OJ Simpson can roll up on a golf course and get a nod and handshake. Yeah, he might have killed a couple of folk, but at least he had once been a card-carrying member of the "acceptable black man" club and in a world overrun by black rappers, drug dealers, and thugs, that still matters for something. Although I'll be the first to admit the need to shepherd a generation of under-achieving, under-prepared, under-appreciative black male youth into a twenty-first century black manhood, I contend that a crisis of black masculinity exists not only in the scapegoated, so-called hip-hop generation, but in the legions of well-adjusted, middle-classed, educated, heterosexual black men, whose continued investment in a powerful American-style patriarchy (often remixed as Black Nationalism and Afrocentrism) and its offspring homophobia, sexism, and misogyny, represents a significant threat to the stability and sustenance of black families, communities, and relationships. Moreover, many of these black men rarely get challenged on these investments, often buffered and protected by black institutions that are themselves buttressed by modes of patriarchal privilege that gets obscured in our quest for achievement, power, and economic stability.

The Hip-Hop Thug versus the New Talented Tenth

Perhaps no one black man captured America's fears and scorn for black men in recent years more than Nushawn Williams.

Embodying the confluence of historic fears among white
Americans about black male sexuality, interracial relationships,
and sexually transmitted diseases, Williams infected over thirteen young women and girls in Jamestown, New York with the
HIV virus between 1996 and 1997. At least half of the women
were infected by Williams *after* he was notified by Chautauqua
County health officials that he had contracted the virus. One of
the girls infected by Williams, who was twenty years old when
the story broke in October of 1997, was thirteen years old
when she had sex with him. During their investigation of the
HIV outbreak, Williams admitted to county health officials that
he had sex with forty-eight women in the county during the
eight-month period he lived in Jamestown, New York. A drug
dealer who had relocated to Jamestown from New York City,
some of Williams's victims were infected in "sex for drugs"
transactions. There is evidence that some of the women and
girls weren't simply infected by unprotected sex, but likely also
by the sharing of the dirty needles they used to take drugs.[3]
Jamestown, New York is a small city of 35,000 residents with
decidedly rural and socially conservative sensibilities, thus the
news of these thirteen women (the thirteen new HIV cases
represented roughly a quarter of all HIV cases reported in
the county over a twenty-year period) was perceived as an
epidemic—literal fear of a viral predator that was threatening
the city's very way of life. That predator was not the disease
itself, but its distributor, Nushawn Williams.

There isn't a shred of ground on which Williams's actions
can be defended (save the fact he was likely as ignorant about
how the HIV virus is spread as the average American) and thus
I have no interest in examining the broader social and cultural
contexts that could even remotely explain Williams's actions.[4]
What I am interested in is examining the media coverage of
Nushawn Williams and how that coverage was informed by
and reproduced historical myths about black men, particularly
black male sexuality. In a culture that has both openly and

privately expressed fear of black male sexuality, whether via mythic fascination with the black male sexual organ and purported black male desire for white women, Nushawn Williams was indeed a giant, diseased, black penis slithering through Smalltown, USA in search of young, nubile white girls.

In the mainstream press, Williams was depicted in ways that consciously and unconsciously referenced common myths about black male sexuality. In a somewhat sympathetic story in the *Washington Post,* Jennifer Frey repeatedly referred to Williams's victims as "Nushawn's Girls," as if he was a pimp who forced these young women and girls out on the street to have unprotected sex.[5] Another portrayed Williams as a "charmer" who through the "apparent lure of drugs and adventure he offered enticed young women into his seedy lair."[6] *Newsweek* made the inevitable link between Williams's appeal and hip-hop culture, stating that "Nobody knows exactly what brought Nushawn Williams to the town, but it is clear that he soon established himself as a relentless seducer of women. He had charm and, to a generation mesmerized by gangsta rap, a menacing form of glamour."[7] In that same story one of the girls admitted that she liked dating "thugs."[8] Chautauqua County health commissioner Dr. Robert Berke told reporters at the *Buffalo News* that Williams was a "score keeper and a very, very good historian," suggesting that his recordkeeping made it easier for officials to track down some of his potential victims.[9] Though many of these comments are innocuous on the surface, it is only when the racial context of Williams's relations with these young women is exhumed that these comments seem to invest in the image of Williams as an oversexualized black man who, endowed with a potent sexuality, had the power to charm even the most innocent of young women and kept a record of his conquests as if he were on some mission to conquer as many white women as possible. As Berke was quoted in a news conference, "he liked to lurk around the edges of school and parks . . . picking out young ladies who may, for one reason or another, be in a risk taking mode."[10]

The racial dynamic of Nushawn Williams was not lost on some commentators. Writing in *USA Today*, Saundra Smokes acknowledges that "If Williams, who is African-American, were accused of infecting African-American teen age girls from urban America rather than white girls from a small, rural town, the story simply would not have been as prominent . . . And if Williams were white, he might not be portrayed as a crazed, HIV-positive 'predator' purposely preying on innocent, troubled young girls, as much as a troubled young man himself."[11] Although she didn't make specific mention of the significance of Williams's race, Ellen Goodman noted in the *Boston Globe* that more attention was given to the "most extreme, deliberate, menacing, even maniacal individual than to the menace itself," later querying, "Do we think that corralling one mad/bad man or two, or two dozen, who maliciously infect unsuspecting partners is an effective public health policy?" Left unspoken in Goodman's analysis of course is the fact that Williams's race made all the difference in the world: it was the reason why everyone was fixated on capturing that one bad man, that one bad nigger. According to political scientist Thomas Shevory, "That Williams was African-American, having sex with teenage white girls, probably transmitting HIV to some of them, in a small town subculture that was infected with drugs, was simply irresistible given the narratives, symbolisms and representations that were (and are) in place. The results were perhaps entirely predictable in terms of the framing of the case."[12]

When a *New York Daily News* editorial described Williams as a "disturbing assortment of social pathologies"—promiscuity, underage sex, unprotected sex, and drugs—it was clear that these attributes were not just inscribed on the body of Williams but on every young black male who could be perceived as the next "Nushawn."[13] If the increased incidence of racial profiling by police and retail outlets has taught us anything, it's that

America has rarely been nuanced in its demonization of black men of all ages, ethnicities, and economic status. Many Americans, particularly those whose perceptions of black masculinity are colored by media portraits, comfortably believe that a significant number of young black man engage in "sexually perverse, predatory behavior (towards) unsuspecting and defenseless victims."[14] Toward the close of the aforementioned *Daily News* editorial, the editors make an effort to position Williams in opposition to former Joint Chief of Staff and Secretary of State Colin Powell, who was quoted from his book *My American Journey*, stating that "We seem to have lost our sense of shame as a society. . . . Nothing seems to embarrass us; nothing shocks us anymore."[15]

The reality is that for men like Powell and those who gathered for the "Who Will Help the Black Man?" session, as well as a good many middle-class, upper-middle-class, and elite black men, the so-called hip-hop thugs and Nushawn Williamses of the world threaten to pull us all back into the abyss of black male demonization. As stories of the racial profiling of "successful" black men such as Hall of Fame baseball player Joe Morgan, publishing executive Earl Graves, Jr., and former NBA player Dee Brown evidence, many black men are all too aware how slippery the slope is from black man to "thug-nigga."[16] The point was powerfully depicted by then-Harvard Law student Bryonn Bain, who gave a first-hand account of racial profiling in *The Village Voice*. The experience led Bain to acknowledge a never-ratified, but "self evident," Bill of Rights for black men in which "Congress can make no law altering the established fact that a black man is a nigger," "The fact that a black Man is a nigger is sufficient and probable cause for him to be searched and seized," and "Wherever niggers are causing trouble, arresting any nigger at the scene of the crime is just as good as arresting the one actually guilty of the crime in question."[17] It shouldn't be surprising then that many black men protect the relative privilege of being black, male, educated, and financially comfortable with a voracity that, in its worst form, creates an animosity toward the image of the hip-hop thug that rivals the animosities expressed by white racists toward blacks.

Given the fact that hip-hop culture has always been male-centered, it is expected that criticisms of it are naturally conflated with criticisms of young black males. In an interview, long-time hip-hop antagonist C. Delores Tucker suggests that the "white music industry has always denigrated the black community. White corporate America has always feared the black male. It wants to suggest black males are inhuman thugs."[18] Tucker also argues that "America is killing off the black male and gangsta rap is one of the weapons."[19] Other commentators cite the negative influence that hip-hop has on the middle-class aspirations of young black men. In their examination of the generational battle within hip-hop culture *Newsweek* noted in passing that as the "number of young black men attending college steadily dwindles . . . the piles of unsolicited demo tapes get higher in record-company offices," a clear indication (in their minds) that many young black men see the road to MTV regular rotation as a more viable route to middle-class success than a college education.[20] Even more explicit is Dr. M. Rick Turner's claim that hip-hop's culture is eroding the numbers of the next generation of the "The Talented Tenth."[21]

The term "talented tenth" was of course posited at the beginning of the twentieth century by noted black scholar and activist W.E.B. Du Bois to describe the formation of an elite, educated, middle-class cadre of folk—black men, essentially—charged to lead the race.[22] Turner, dean of African-American Affairs at the University of Virginia, voices concern that black male students at the university—part of a future "talented tenth"—who "come from affluent backgrounds" and are "increasingly second-generation college students . . . often fail to become involved in many aspects of university life."[23] Turner adds that "Our young black men haven't always behaved this way." He later comes to the conclusion that he suspects that those young men "lack incentives to get involved. But could it be that the consumption of music—particularly hip-hop—has taken too many of our black boys away from the realities of life?"[24] Of course Turner's assessment has some validity, though there are myriad reasons why black students recoil from campus activities, including some discomfort with the lily-whiteness of some campuses or the recognition as second-generation college students (in those cases), privy to the experiences of their parents, that all that awaits them upon graduation in corporate America is a glass ceiling.

But what is of interest to me about Turner's comments is his willing embrace of a stridently patriarchal notion of the "talented tenth." The social conventions of the early twentieth century, can explain, but not justify, the absence of women in much of Du Bois's conception of the "talented tenth," however, Turner's comment subtly reflects the continued investment among "successful black men" in forms of patriarchy and the top-shelf, publicly sanitized sexism and misogyny that comes with expressions of black male privilege. At the same time that Turner constructs an image of hip-hop generation black males that is clearly out of sync with his notion of the "talented tenth"—the proverbial "strong black man"—he also embraces an archaic notion of black masculinity that notably ignores how black women, even those on his campus, "contribute out-standing leadership to the black community."[25] In the minds of Turner, and I would argue far too many black men of his ilk, the unwillingness of young black men to embrace a "talented tenth" ethos is tantamount to a crisis. Said another way, these young black men, the hip-hop generation, are being held accountable for not embracing sanitized, institutionally accept-able forms of black patriarchy. Lost in much of this process is that the very sexism, homophobia, and misogyny that circulates within hip-hop culture and becomes part of the context in which black males of the hip-hop generation are demonized within the mainstream, are expressions of the very same patriarchy that the so-called "talented tenth" posit as part of a normative and necessary black masculinity. Two separate incidents over the last decade or so highlight how this situation has played out in the mainstream.

In 1993 Reverend Calvin O. Butts, III led a very public campaign against so-called "gangsta rap," culminating in the steamrolling of hundreds of rap CDs in front of Harlem's Abyssinian Baptist Church, where he was head pastor. Butts's campaign smacked of political opportunism and he was dutifully accused of advocating censorship of rap lyrics,[26] though in his defense, he was recreating the symbolic role that black audiences played in segregated entertainment venues in the past, by weeding out material that was not in the best interests of the community or at least containing that material within the confines of black life.[27] What was interesting about Butts's campaign is the way that it was framed as an effort to protect black women. Not surprisingly, Butts announced his campaign in Abyssinian's pulpit on Mother's Day of 1993. In subsequent interviews he stated that "It is not helpful to have black women bumping and grinding their almost-bare buttocks," and later rhetorically queried, "How are we going to talk about stopping violence against women and children abuse when you've got it there in these videos?"[28] In a separate interview, C. Vernon Mason, a noted civil rights lawyer and deacon at Abyssinian, affirmed Butts's efforts, offering that "The overwhelming majority of people in our community are not in favor of our women being referred to as bitches."[29] Given the concerns of Butts and Mason about the well-being of black women, one has to wonder why Butts didn't steamroll the collection plates of those black churches who engage in forms of sexism against black women and who remain silent when their ministers prey on women within the confines of those churches.[30]

Anti-violence activist Frances E. Wood writes that "Within the African-American church community the silence about the realities of women's experience and how it differs from men's experience has taken on the proportions of a version of the 'big lie,' and is a deadly yoke. This yoke consist of silencing, ignoring, degrading, and dismissing women's experience, especially those experiences that reveal the nature and extent of oppression perpetrated within the (church) community."[31] For example, when John Carter, a black minister in the United Methodist Church was charged and convicted of sexually harassing five women (two white and three black), fellow clergy Reverend Lovell Parham, at the time a campus minister at historically black Howard University, asserted that the "women clergy have become our enemy."[32] Very often, black women themselves vehemently protect the very black ministers who prey on them in the church. After one of the black women plaintiffs testified, she was confronted by several other black women, who, suspecting that there was some kind of racist conspiracy against Carter, demanded to know, "Who paid you to testify? How much?"[33] According to feminist scholar Candace Jenkins, the desire of those who confronted the plaintiff to close ranks with other figures like Carter is "part of a pattern of black desire that I call the 'salvific wish.' The salvific wish is best understood as an aspiration, most often but not only middle-class and female, to save or rescue the black community from white racist accusations of sexual and domestic pathology, through conventional bourgeois propriety."[34]

It perhaps goes without saying the likelihood of Carter's conviction was significantly increased because of the involvement of two white plaintiffs. In the context of religious institutions that are still largely segregated along racial lines, sexual predators within the black church don't receive the same scrutiny within mainstream culture. And the desire among black men and women within the black church to keep the sexual politics of the black church behind closed doors often encourages sexist behavior by black ministers, who don't have to fear mainstream embarrassment or censure. Discussing the sexual

politics of the black church, ordained minister Marcia L. Dyson
admits to the "undeniable power that the men in our pulpits
have over the women in the pulpits. And too many times I've
seen preachers exploit this power and even take it for granted,
as if it were an entitlement."[35] Making a connection between
the men in the pulpit and those on the street, Dyson adds,
"Let's face it: The bravado and machismo of many male ministers link them to their secular brethren. 'You know all she
needs is a good [fuck]' echoes not just on the streets, around
the watercooler or in the army barracks—it's heard even in the
pastor's study."[36] Dyson also notes how black male sexual privilege within the church informs some of the ministers' opinions
about homosexuality, recalling a conversation with a lesbian
theology student who after confiding to her minister about her
sexuality, was told that she needed "straightening out" and that
he was the "man to do it."[37] The point here is that attempts
by church and civic leaders like Calvin Butts and others to protect black women from the threat of "gangsta rap" ring hollow
when they remain silent about the kinds of protection that black
women need in their own churches.

In another well-publicized incident, the civil rights old guard,
led by Reverend Jesse Jackson, Sr. and Reverend Al Sharpton,
took issue with comments made by a character in the film
Barbershop. The character, portrayed by Cedric the Entertainer, in an exchange with patrons and employees in a Chicago
barbershop, suggests that civil-rights-era matriarch Rosa Parks,
whose principled stand against segregating seating on buses in
Montgomery, Alabama is legendary, "Ain't do nothin' but sit her
black ass down." Later in the film he refers to the Dr. Reverend
Martin Luther King, Jr. as a "ho" (a black colloquialism for
"whore"), later suggesting that on "Martin Luther King's birthday, I want everybody to take the day off and get your freak on."
When one of the other characters warns Cedric the Entertainer's
character that his comments might attract the attention and
scorn of Jesse Jackson, Sr., he responds, "Fuck Jesse Jackson."

Negative responses to the comments were swift. The film starred actor and hip-hop artist Ice Cube and given its clear hip-hop-centric themes, it was easily implicated as another example of the failings of the hip-hop generation.

In an editorial, Anthony King chided Cedric the Entertainer for his "flippant disrespect for our civil rights heroes" and his comments as "reflective of a generation that has lost touch with its legacy and lacks cultural respect."[38] He later admonished the hip-hop generation, "Please leave our black heroes alone."[39] In an interview with *USA Today*, Reverend Jackson voiced his concern that the "filmmakers crossed the line between what's sacred and serious and what's funny."[40] Ever the politician, Jackson attempted to distance his own personal interests in the film's commentary stating that "I could dismiss the comments about me. . . . But Dr. King is dead, and Mrs. Parks is an invalid."[41] In classic Jackson mode, he claimed to speak for the dead and unable, effectively using the damage done to King's and Park's images as a media pulpit for himself. Though he claims to not speak for himself, one can surmise that what really got at Jackson was the "fuck Jesse Jackson" quip, because it articulated the increased sense among blacks that he was irrelevant as a political leader. According to William Jelani Cobb, the controversy over *Barbershop* "illustrated how far things have devolved: faced with unchecked military aggression, a White House that has a renewed and overt commitment to imperialism, a million incarcerated African Americans and a national conscience bereft of moral considerations, Jesse and company were left to film criticism as a form of protest."[42] Was coming to the defense of a "dead" King and an "invalid" Parks really an attempt to defend black heroes or was it an attempt to protect the images of black patriarchal privilege such as those expressed by Reverend Jackson and Reverend King at various points in their public careers?

At the time that Jackson and others (including Parks herself and the King family) began to complain about the depictions of

King and Parks in the film, Mary Mitchell noted that "When Rosa Parks was mugged by a black teenager several years ago, that was something to get angry about."[43] According to Mitchell while "civil rights leaders shook their heads in disgust, little was done to express Black America's outrage," later derisively adding, "Now African Americans are supposed to be outraged over a movie? I don't think so."[44] Mitchell's analysis suggests that Jackson's protests had little to do with Rosa Parks. In this regard, the film's critique of Reverend King as a philanderer is important as Reverend Jackson's own public admission of an extramarital affair and fathering of an "illegitimate" child was brought back into focus.[45] Although King's own philandering was fairly well known within civil rights' circles, the openness with which the film confronted this reality threatened his iconical status as a moral crusader among those not privy to his sexual history. Both Jackson and King were products of black church culture and the black patriarchy that it emboldens. Michael Eric Dyson suggests that "as surely as King learned from the black church the use of brilliant rhetorical strategies that would help change America, and as surely as he was shaped in its crucible of biblical interpretations of social sin and suffering, he learned in the same setting about the delights of the flesh that were formally forbidden but were in truth the sweet reward of spiritual servants."[46] No doubt the film's screenwriter Mark Brown, whose credits include *How to Be a Player* (1997) and *Two Can Play that Game* (2001), was cognizant of that fact when he placed the two men in close proximity in the film. My point in discussing these incidents is to suggest that the "talented tenth" often use criticisms of the hip-hop generation to mask their own infidelities and investments in patriarchal practices that are also damaging to the black community.

In the catalogue for the exhibition *Black Male: Representations of Masculinity in Contemporary American Art*, Thelma Golden, the exhibition's curator, writes that "One of the greatest inventions of the twentieth century is the African-American

male—invented because black masculinity represents an amal- ⟋
gam of fears and projections in the American psyche which
rarely conveys or contains the trope of truth about the black
male's existence."[47] In that same volume Clyde Taylor states
that "Black men are densely mythogenic, the object of layered
fictions produced by others. . . . And like other mythogenic
people, Black men are, as if in self-defense, prolific generators
of self-descriptive legends."[48] Image-making among elite black
men dates back to the early twentieth century when black men
like W.E.B. Du Bois, Alain Locke, and others began to circulate terms like the "talented tenth" and the "new negro" in an
effort to challenge racist depictions of black folk, but black men
in particular.[49] These were "positive" and "strong" constructions
of black masculinity that would directly counter images of the
shuffling Sambo or blackface caricatures of black men by white
minstrel performers. As historian Kevin Gaines suggests, minstrelsy was a particularly damaging phenomenon for black elites
because it "mocked the elite aspirations of African-Americans. . . .
Its objective was often to undermine transgressive images of
black power and equality."[50]

Even today words like Sambo and minstrel are used by the
"talented tenth" to describe hip-hop. In response to protest
over a board game that negatively depicted life in the ghetto,
Joseph H. Brown suggests that the game's creator David Chang
would have to "sell a lot of games to earn the money 50 Cent,
Jay Z [prominent hip-hop artists] and others have made putting
on a modern day minstrel show."[51] Gaines notes that during
the early twentieth century, "Racist minstrel and journalistic
discourses trumpeted images of absent patriarchy as evidence
of black inferiority," and "Black nationalist intellectuals, haunted
by the memory of slavery and its destruction of the family,
restricted their idea of the race's oppression to the terms dic-
tated by minstrelsy."[52] Given Gaines's analysis, it's not surprising
that calls to reclaim black patriarchy—to reclaim the family—
began to reach a fever pitch just as hip-hop became one of the

most prominent vehicles by which mainstream culture viewed black life and culture. It is my contention that much like those first-generation "new negroes," today's successful black men— the contemporary "talented tenth"—often engage in their own forms of myth-making and image management in order to protect the privilege they derive in mainstream America (relative to white men of course) and more important, the privilege and power they wield within black social, political, cultural, and religious institutions. The grandest example of this occurred on October 16, 1995.

There's a New Black Man in America Today

It was hailed as the greatest gathering of black men ever and the greatest public gathering of black folk since the March on Washington in August of 1963. According to its organizers, the Million Man March (1995) was to "declare to the world our readiness to stand up like free Black men to take responsibility of the freedom allegedly given to us in 1865."[53] More specifically Nation of Islam leader Louis Farrakhan and march organizers viewed the day of the Million Man March, October 16, 1995, as a "Holy Day of Atonement and Reconciliation" for black men. In advance of the historic march Farrakhan wrote, "We, as men, must atone for the abuse of our women and girls, and our failure to be leaders of and builders of our community. . . . We must atone for the destruction that is going on within our communities; the fratricide, the death dealing drugs, and the violence that plagues us."[54] On the surface Farrakhan's call for atonement spoke to the need for those black men engaged in acts of criminality, violence, and blatant misogyny to own up to the damage that they do within the black community. This spirit was also expressed in the "Million Man March Pledge" that Farrakhan asked the black men in attendance to repeat: "I pledge this day forward I will never abuse my wife by striking her, disrespecting her, for she is the mother of my children and the producer of my future. I pledge from this day forward

I will never engage in the abuse of children, little boys or little girls for sexual gratification. . . . I will never again use the 'B word' to describe any female. But particularly my own black sister."[55] Although Farrakhan's pledge seemed to represent an act of black male self-critique, it was clear that Farrakhan's appeal was not to the average black male in attendance, but to some of the more demonic male forces within the black community.

In her commentary on the march Debra Dickerson noted the aura of politeness and chivalry she experienced walking through the crowd of black men: "Paths opened before us; chairs appeared from nowhere; men yanked their sons aside saying, 'boy, let your auntie by.' For an entire day I was 'auntie,' I was 'sister,' I was 'daughter.' Not 'bitch,' not 'ho,' not 'sweet thang.'"[56] Indeed, Dickerson's sense that she was "queen for a day" suggests that there was an element of performance taking place that day, as if black men were performing for an international media, corporate America, and their wives, sisters, mothers, aunts, daughters, girlfriends, and grandmothers who were asked by the march's organizers to stay at home the day of the march. Dickerson was part of a small percentage of black women in attendance at the march that day. The march organizers explicitly told black women and girls—"our women and girls"—"you have been so patient waiting for us to take up our responsibility; so now that we have made up our minds to stand up for you and our families, we want you to aid us in this march by *staying home with the children teaching them in sympathy with what Black men have decided to do* [my emphasis]."[57]

Undeniably, the Million Man March's spiritual figurehead at various times in his public career lived up to Dickerson's claim that the Nation of Islam leader espoused "anti-Semitic, anti-intellectual, sexist and homosexual-baiting racism."[58] Although many of the men who supported the march were quick to distance themselves from Farrakhan's perceived anti-Semitism, few ventured to distance themselves from the minister's regular

forays into sexist and homophobic rhetoric. Literary scholar
Houston A. Baker Jr. observes that "Many who assembled on
the Mall knew the Minister would articulate—publicly and at
a globally televised symbolic site—their own discontent. Such
public articulation they felt was cathartic and necessary, indeed,
indispensable—because most black men don't have country
clubs or country-club estates in gated communities, or unli-
censed authority and secretiveness in which to batter their
wives and desert their children in the name of 'job stress' like
so many white men do."[59]

Given this psychic and sentimental connection to the shared
pain of being black and male in American society, few of the
march's supporters took the opportunity to challenge the retrograde patriarchal goals of the Million Man March in the
way that members of Men Stopping Violence, an Atlanta-based
organization dedicated to ending men's violence against women,
did. In a letter addressed to Farrakhan, members of Men Stopping Violence urged him to "consider the physical, mental and
spiritual consequences of reinforcing the notion that Black
men intend to 'take over' the leadership of families which *the
conditions of this system* have not allowed us to share."[60] Black
gay men were reticent about the march because of Farrakhan's
well-known homophobic views, including a 1984 diatribe in
which he suggested that a "sissified" Michael Jackson "projects
to young black men . . . an image that we all should reject."[61]
Reflecting the well-founded belief among black gay men and
others that the Million Man March's aims teetered on blatant
homophobia, Robert Reid-Pharr writes, "If the real message
of the march was that it is going to take heroic black masculinity to restore order to our various communities . . . then it
follows that black gay men are irrelevant, or even dangerous, to
that project."[62]

Two incidents further affirmed the concerns of black gay
and bisexual men about the heterosexist's goals of the march
and even their safety, if they chose to march alongside their

heterosexual brothers. In one case, Nation of Islam Minister William 3X, head of Mosque #3 in Milwaukee, admitted that black gay men were welcome but only if "they are willing to atone for *their* sins [my emphasis] as we are going to atone for our own."[63] More pointedly Minister William 3X stated, "We are atoning for our sins and homosexuality is an abomination in the eyes of God, just as fornication, abuse of women and children are sins," adding that "If they are proud of their homosexuality and not willing to make a change and not willing to make atonement, then they are not coming to the march in the right spirit."[64] In this case Minister William 3X employs a classic rhetorical move in which religious texts, in this case the Koran, is used to shroud nefarious practices such as slavery, domination of women, and homophobic rhetoric that borders on rhetorical violence that can easily be used to justify real physical violence against black gay men.

Lost on Minister William 3X is the fact that black gay men can be and are productive citizens of black communities, fathers, brothers, partners, and a host of other things supposedly embodied in the "strong black man." Minister William 3X's myopic view of black homosexuals is premised on a dichotomy in which the black homosexual is viewed as "soft" and unmanly and thus in opposition to the hard "strong black man." This view was powerfully expressed when Bishop George Augustus Stallings of the Imani Temple and a supporter of the march, deflected criticisms of Farrakhan with the vile homophobic retort, "What do you want, some milquetoast, sissy faggot to lead you to the promised land?"[65] As law professor Kendall Thomas reflected at the time in response to figures like Minister William 3X and Bishop Stallings, "There are dirty hands all around the organizing committee of this march; men who have made violent hateful remarks. There are people associated with this march who are committed to our extinction."[66]

Black women who spoke out about the march's gender apartheid and nostalgia for patriarchy were accordingly demonized.

Economist and commentator Julianne Malveaux was one of many prominent black women writers and activists who were critical of the march, including bell hooks, Angela Davis, Michele Wallace, Pearl Cleage, and legal scholar Kimberle Crenshaw. According to Malveaux, "My car was vandalized several times after I made some negative remarks about the Nation of Islam and Farrakhan. . . . And for a while my phone calls were dominated by black men shouting personal insults."[67] In response to the legitimate critiques of the march by black feminists, black political scientist Robert Starks stated, "These black feminists are criticizing exactly what most black women in our communities want: strong men," also noting that in the "Robert Taylor Homes (in Chicago), for example, nearly 90 percent of the apartments are occupied by poor single women and their children. They desperately want Patriarchy."[68]

Starks seemed to be oblivious to the fact that black women may themselves embrace debilitating forms of black patriarchy simply because there are few other options in a society that posits the patriarchal family as the norm and often interprets the failure of the black community to embody that normalcy as the fault of black women. Referring again to the work of Candace Jenkins, she notes that the "salvific wish has most influenced female behavior because it has historically placed a high value on maintaining a protective illusion of black sexual and familial sobriety. This illusion is particularly dependent upon (and prohibitive for) black women because the black female body has so often been characterized as the sole source of black intimate or domestic irregularity"[69] In other words the desire for some black women to have a more viable patriarchal presence in their life is not just about closing ranks with black men, but ironically, sanitizing their own images, in the face of willful demonization by mainstream culture ("welfare queens") and black men ("baby mama drama" and "chickenheads").[70] Starks seems equally oblivious to the fact that what these women in the Robert Taylor Houses and elsewhere may have wanted are not retrograde patriarchs, but *partners*, who *shared* child-rearing, domestic, and wage-earning responsibilities with them.

"There's a New Black Man in America today," Farrakhan exhorted on the day of the Million Man March. I was one of the many black men who stayed at home that day, though less out of the conviction of closing ranks with my feminist sisters who challenged the march's ideals and more so out of a profound conflict over which camp I belonged to. I watched much of the march in the apartment of one of my best friends (we embraced at some point when overcome with the emotion of the day) and later explained to my students that I thought it was irresponsible as a black man not to fulfill my duties as their instructor that night, hence my decision not to go to the march. Nearly a decade later, I'm clear about which camp I'm in. It is now clear to me, that when the march organizers stated to "our women and girls" that "If all of us will unite this one day, then the world will take notice that there is a new Black man in America" they weren't really calling for a "new black man," but for a public coronation of the same old black male patriarch that has been at the root of black male dysfunction, be it the hip-hop generation or the talented tenth.[71] They were calling for the rebirth of a figure I'll just call the "Strong Black Man," a figure that was a product of the imaginations of both the talented-tenth and rabid black nationalists and Afrocentrists alike.

The "Strong Black Man" is the flagship product of nearly 400 years of lived experiences by black men in North America, black men who in the process of resisting enslavement, economic exploitation, random and calculated violence, and a host of other afflictions that usually befall those with a foot on their neck, created a functional myth on which the black nation could be built. The "Strong Black Man" is represented by seminal race men such as Martin Delaney, Fredrick Douglas, W.E.B. Du Bois, and Marcus Garvey, who spoke truth to power about racism and black disenfranchisement. Maurice O. Wallace's exhaustive study of the imagery of African-American men is useful in understanding just how the "Strong Black Man" was literally constructed in the eighteenth and nineteenth centuries. Wallace cites portraits of Prince Hall (founder of the Prince Hall Masons) and Martin Delaney as "models of black exceptionalism to be emulated by other black Masons and respectable African American men."[72] The portraits of Hall and Delaney appeared in 1903 (125 years after Hall's death) and in 1865, respectively, and thus had an impact on the generations of "race men" who existed at the time as the portraits offered "visual models of the sort of 'disciplinary individualism' and black masculine perfectibility the earliest Masons purposed to preserve ritualistically."[73]

Delaney is well known as the "father" of black nationalism on the strength of his tome *The Condition, Elevation, Emigration and Destiny of the Colored People of the United States Politically Considered* (1852). It is important that he was also influenced by Prince Hall's legacy as he was the first Freemason in the United States to publish a history of the Prince Hall craft. After leaving the United States in the early 1850s, Delaney returned during the Civil War to support the efforts of eradicating slavery. He was commissioned as a major in the Union army in 1865 and it was in this context that Delaney posed for a portrait in uniform. According to Wallace, the Delaney portrait "came to portray not an exceptional man but a typical one, general and reproducible by others. The carte distilled broad, black masculine ambition into a single image and helped shape a specific form of black masculine ideality."[74] In other words, Delaney's portrait became the visual template for an emerging generation of "Strong Black Men" including Booker T. Washington, Alexander Crummell, and even W.E.B. Du Bois. Although elements of Delaney's early ruminations on black nationalism would survive well into the twentieth century, when a distinct form of black nationalism re-emerged in the context of the Black Power movement, it could best be described by what Norm R. Allen, Jr., calls "Reactionary Black Nationalism." According to Allen, "On the one hand, Reactionary Black Nationalists advocate self-love, self-respect, self-acceptance, self-help, pride, unity"—all valuable and needed attributes for members of black communities and institutions—but also promote "bigotry, intolerance, hatred, sexism [and] homophobia" among other things.[75] It is this "Reactionary Black Nationalism" that informs the "Strong Black Man" of the 1960s (and beyond) and animates political figures such as Elijah Muhammad, Maulana Karenga, Louis Farrakhan, Stokely Carmichael (Kwame Toure), Malcolm X (el-hajj Malik el-Shabazz), Amiri Baraka, and Eldridge Cleaver at various stages in their careers.

The most negative aspects of the "Strong Black Man" of the 1960s are perhaps best embodied in the figure of Cleaver, who became a popular icon of the era on the basis of his best-selling autobiography *Soul on Ice* (1968). Written while Cleaver was a prisoner in Folsom State Prison in California, the book was hailed as a "spiritual and intellectual autobiography that stands at the exact resonant center of the new Negro writing."[76] According to such logic then, sentiments such as Cleaver's assertion that "rape was an insurrectionary act" that he refined, not on the white women, who were his political targets, but "black girls in the ghetto" would also be at the "exact" center of the fermenting black masculinity of the period espoused by Cleaver and the like.[77] Not totally satisfied with relishing his misogyny, Cleaver later shares this now-famous homophobic ditty that the "white man has deprived" the black homosexual of his "masculinity" and "castrated him in the center of his burning skull."[78] James Baldwin was the specific target of Cleaver's attacks, but his homophobic rant resonated powerfully among many black men regarding the impact of homosexuality in the black community. Years later Cleaver is still held in high regard largely on the basis of his stance on American race relations, and his misogyny and homophobia are largely ignored or seen as excusable in a world where "race" often trumps "gender" and "sexuality" as meaningful issues within the black community.

As someone who once aspired to be a "Strong Black Man," I understand that most of those men who I aspired to be like always had a real love of black folk. So yes, "The Strong Black Man" is a defender of black femininity—one who *publicly* treats black women in a chivalrous nature like that historically afforded to white women. And yes, "The Strong Black Man" is also a provider—providing the primary financial support for his family as well as stability, honor, and discipline for his children, particularly in a society that has historically deemed black men as lazy, shiftless, indifferent, and parasitic. But as Allen suggests, despite seemingly positive attributes, the figure of the "Strong Black Man" can be faulted for championing a stunted, conservative, one-dimensional, and stridently heterosexual vision of black masculinity that has little to do with the vibrant, virile, visceral masculinities that are lived in the real world. Black masculinities that are often masked—the DLs (on the down low homosexuals who live as heterosexuals) immediately come to mind—in the name of living up to the mythical "Strong Black Man." Some of these so-called "Strong Black Men" have at times been unrepentant in their sexism, misogyny, and homophobia. But somehow when our mythical black nation is under siege and in crisis, the only thing that is not allowable, especially when at war, is the demise of the "Strong Black Man." And according to some pundits (both the organizational and the barbershop variety) the black man is *always* at war—at war with "the white man," at war with "the system," and at war with *his woman*, the black woman. To some, to acknowledge some of these shortcomings or to scrutinize these men and hold "some damn body" accountable, is to attack the "Strong Black Man" and thus attack the very foundation of the black nation. Even worse, it's an attempt to collude with our enemies to bring down the race. Whatever.

The "Strong Black Man" was conceived as the ultimate counter to the distorted images of shiftless, shuffling, threatening, and dangerous black men that populated virtually every facet of American public and commercial culture, and thus the image of the "Strong Black Man" is maintained at all cost. Many of the black male narratives of the last decade or so, including Nathan McCall's *Makes Me Wanna Holler*, Haki Madhubuti's *Tough Notes: Letters to Young Black Men*, and Ellis Cose's *The Envy of the World: On Being a Black Man in America*, were conceived as an effort to buttress the very idea of the "Strong Black Man" within the context in what has seemed as a three-decade-long crusade on "saving the black man." A crusade, I might add, often coordinated by hackneyed civil rights organizations and their self-anointed HNICs (head niggas in charge). Many have been inspired by Daniel Patrick Moynihan's study "The Negro Family: The Case for National Action." Written while Moynihan was Assistant Secretary of Labor during President Lyndon Johnson's administration, the report stated that in the aftermath of the passage of the Civil Rights Act of 1964 blacks would "expect that in the near future equal opportunities for them as a group will produce roughly equal results, as compared with other groups. This is not going to happen. Nor will it happen for generations to come unless a new and special effort is made." According to Moynihan, the "fundamental problem . . . is that of family structure."[79] Specifically the so-called "tangle of pathology" that afflicts the black community is a "matriarchal structure which, because it is so out of line with the rest of the American society, seriously retards the progress of the group as a whole and imposes a *crushing burden* [my emphasis] on the Negro male."[80]

In what should be regarded as a well-worn quote by now, Moynihan further argued that American society "presumes male leadership in private and public affairs. The arrangements of society facilitate such leadership and reward it. A subculture, such as that of the Negro American, in which this is not the

pattern, is placed at a distinct disadvantage."[81] In one bold stroke,
78 pages in length, Moynihan essentially argued that "Negro"
acceptance into the mainstream of American life was premised
on the embrace of patriarchy. When elements of Moynihan's
report were included in President Johnson's historic address
at the Howard University commencement in June of 1965, the
President and Assistant Secretary (who co-wrote the address)
became unwitting collaborators with the '60s-styled "Strong
Black Man." Even if the black power fists, afros, and dashikis
have gone the way of any fad, Moynihan's critique of the black
family continues to inform contemporary thinking about the
plight of black men. Gotta let a man be a man. In the decades
that have followed since Daniel Moynihan's notorious report
on the black family, which for all intents suggested that black
men were punks, it's as if every five minutes there's another
"save the black man" conference or pamphlet. The Million Man
March in 1995 was just the grandest of those efforts.

   For damn sure the black man is under siege, but it's not as
if the saving of the black man should come at the expense of
black women and children who continue to be under siege
also, often at the hands of so-called "Strong Black Men." Thus
desires to save black men and protect the most powerful of
them has had damaging consequences to the black community
as figures like Reverend Henry Lyons, Mike Tyson, hip-hop artists Dr. Dre, singer R. Kelly, and Reverend Jesse Jackson have
been given "save the black man" passes for some straight-up,
damaging behavior such as extra-marital affairs (as was the case
with the two reverends), rape, assault, embezzlement, and in
the case of Kelly alleged sexual relations with young girls and
child pornography. Of course there are distinctions here according to class and vocations of said black men, so that Tyson or
Kelly were not extended the same benefit of the doubt afforded
Jackson or Lyons (protected by the cloth), although events like
the "Welcome Home from Jail" parade for Tyson, who was
convicted of raping eighteen-year-old Desiree Washington in

1992 would suggest otherwise. On the eve of Tyson's release in 1995 a group of black men including former presidential candidate Al Sharpton, Harlem Congressman Rangel, and promoter Don King, among others, planned a homecoming celebration— a hero's welcome on the real—for the boxer, to which noted black writer Jill Nelson responded, "Over my dead body. . . . Not while I'm living here."[82] In another example, even as many in the black community condemned R. Kelly for being a sexual predator among teenage girls, the bootlegged copy of Kelly's "sexcapades" would have been number one on the Amazon.com list, if they kept track of bootleg sales. When Kelly released *The Chocolate Factory* (2003) months after being indicted on twenty-one counts of child pornography, the recording debuted at number one on the pop charts and he was afforded numerous awards for the recording including Black Entertainment Television's (BET) Male R&B "Artist of the Year."

However good the intentions of its creation, the "Strong Black Man" unfortunately helps reinforce a rigid model of black masculinity that allows for little if any flexibility. In this context, models of black masculinity that ventured too far beyond the "Strong Black Man" are seen as suspect: not quite black enough, not quite man enough, not quite blackman enough. There have been books dealing with black male gay identity such as Thomas Glave's brilliant collection of short stories *Whose Song?* and Robert F. Reid-Pharr's *Black Gay Man,* that have championed more progressive ideas about black male sexuality. In *Black Gay Man,* Reid-Pharr offers his own radical vision of black masculinity in the provocative essay "Living as a Lesbian." Paying tribute to black lesbian thinkers and artists such as Cheryl Clarke (whose book *Living as a Lesbian* inspired Reid-Pharr's essay), Audre Lorde, Barbara Smith, and Cheryl Dunye, Reid-Pharr argues that to "become myself, I have to become a lesbian."[83] According to the author, the value of his "living as a lesbian" is that he is forced to be "committed to the process of constantly becoming, of creatively refashioning one's humanity as a matter of course."[84] In this instance, Reid-Pharr posits a black masculinity that is fluid and malleable, a masculinity that challenges the rigid and truncated versions of black masculinity that masquerade in the bodies of the pro-verbial "strong black man." Although the work of black gay male writers such as Glave, Reid-Pharr, and others such as scholars E. Patrick Johnson, Dwight McBride, and artists such as the late poet Essex Hemphill and the late filmmaker Marlon Riggs have been invaluable to those within the black com-munity seeking alternative models of black masculinity, there have been few heterosexual black male writers who have been willing to embrace the gray areas of black masculinity in ways that collapse rigid perceptions of black heterosexual identity.

The post–civil-rights era has witnessed a relative explosion of what I call black meta-identities, a diversity of black identi-ties that under the logic of segregated America, remained under wraps, mentioned in hushed tones like the crackhead uncle that nobody wants to talk about. And yes, for some black folks, women who embraced strident woman-centered blackness or those black bodies who poked and prodded the rigid hetero-sexist norms of the black community were, like the crackhead uncle, in need of some kind of rehabilitation. While so many aspects of black identity have flourished in the post–civil-rights era, allowing for rich and diverse visions of blackness, black masculinity has remained one aspect of black identity still in need of a radical reconstruction. ("Bruh, just because you takin' care of yo' kids, and don't call their mama a "bitch" and wear condoms when you on the DL and ain't never hit a woman, don't mean you doin' anything significant.") It is my intent to rescue Farrakhan's "New Black Man" from the claws of old-school black male patriarchy.

NewBlackMan is about resisting being inscribed by a wide range of forces and finding a comfort with a complex and pro-gressive existence as a black man in America. As such, *New-BlackMan* is not so much about conceiving of a more "positive" version of black masculinity—"positive" being a word too often used by the traditional black bourgeoisie to sanitize the more unsightly aspects of black life and culture (see the NAACP Image Awards)—but rather a concept that acknowledges the many complex aspects, often contradictory, that make up a progressive and meaningful black masculinity. The words "new," "black," and "man," are literally scrunched together here to reinforce the idea that myriad identities exist in the same black male bodies: in my case the thug-nigga-intellectual, the homeboy-feminist, the recovering homophobe, the doting daddy of two brown-skinned little girls, the loving husband, and the God-fearing thirty-something black man who damn sure appreciates a fine ass on a woman. *NewBlackMan* has precedent in the famous black bodies of Harlem-based poets, modern geniuses of soul and jazz, Marxist organizers who had the ear of a civil rights King, visionary filmmakers, and a host of other not-so-famous black men who had a comfort in their masculinity, even as those who ostensibly looked like them held them to scorn for not being man enough, not being black enough, and not being blackman enough. *NewBlackMan* is for those willing to embrace the fuzzy edges of a black masculinity that in reality is still under construction. As I said in the Introduction, the concept of *NewBlackMan* can be best captured in a line from the HBO film *Boycott* where Bayard Rustin (Erik Todd Dellums) says, "I am a man of my times, but the times don't know it yet!"

New Black Man is my attempt to lay out some of the contours of this evolving progressive black masculinity, as those contours are informed by my own experiences as a hip-hop-generation intellectual. The idea of the *NewBlackMan* may be predicated on seeing black masculinity as something that is fluid, but it's also a dance with contradictions or "fucking with grays," as Joan Morgan talks about it in her book *When Chick-enheads Come Home to Roost*. One of the tensions throughout this book is the question of how willing am I to undermine my status within traditional black masculinity by claiming politics that most "Strong Black Men" would consider the politics of a "punk-ass"? Thus *New Black Man* draws from my experiences in the classroom as a professor, as a writer who engages black popular culture, black feminist thought, and black queer studies, and lastly as a father and husband, who at times struggles with living up to the progressive claims that I often make in my writings and in my classroom.

Chapter 2

what the hell is a black male feminist?

Sons—boys have no role models—Our girls have us as positive role models—the boys have nothing—they are trail blazers—they are making their own definition of self as men.

Audre Lorde[1]

There is no blueprint that exists to help produce young black men in America who are even remotely sensitive to the differing realities of women, particularly black women, and especially if those young black men are asked to venture beyond the most simplistic and obvious markers of gender difference. And of course as part of a community of folk struggling within a racist and racially defined society, there was rarely an instance when we even remotely thought about how gender, or even sexuality, complicated the experience of those of us who weren't

male. Because my father—a strong black man in his own right—
often marked his worth to me as a father and as a man in the
larger society with the number of hours he put in at work (trying to create some semblance of lower middle-class existence
for his family), homie was a real ghost throughout much of my
youth. Not that I begrudged his absence. I always understood
he was hustling the only way he knew how and the only way he
could with a tenth-grade education. What it meant was that my
mother was the most imposing figure in my life, courtesy of her
constant presence in my daily life and her forceful personality.

Thus from a young age I, on some level, viewed life through
the eyes of this black woman who chased bourgeois dreams,
agonized over the utter inability of my father to ever find value
in those dreams, and *always* thought that it was important that
she be heard. Was my mother a feminist? The thought never
occurred to me, even now it doesn't, though if being the most
imposing 4'11" black woman I had ever confronted was a crite-
rion, I would have to say she was. My mother went to work
full-time when I began grade school, purposely taking a job as
a school lunch helper (she only had two years of college at the
time) so that she could be home when I got home from school.
On those days when she couldn't pick me up from school, I was
picked up by "Ms. Bo," a lovely, gracious, and stylish older
black woman, who owned the beauty shop next door to the
tenement building I lived in. And there I sat in her beauty
shop at least once a week eavesdropping on the lives, loves,
dreams, fears of black women of every hue, shape, class, hair
texture, and of course soaking up all the love and affection that
a room full of black women can give, especially when you're
the only male shortie in the room. If I could answer Michael
Eric Dyson's rhetorical question *Why I Love Black Women?* it's
because I was exposed to the full range and nuances of black
female beauty and strength, literally from the time I could identify my ABCs.

My first crush was on my second-grade teacher, one of the six black women teachers—Ms. Miller, Ms. Goodine, Ms. Riley, Mrs. Armstrong, Mrs. Phipps, Mrs. Karr—who shepherded me through my first eight years of schooling and were virtually the only black teachers I would see in over 20 years of formal schooling, excepting a high-school English teacher and the black woman who would become my intellectual mentor as a graduate student. If the women of Muriel Bolding's beauty parlor were there to give a little brown-skinned boy some affectionate affirmation, the black women of the R.T. Hudson Seventh Day Adventist School in the Bronx were there to dispense discipline, academic rigor, and an uncommon sense of moral decency. Though I thrived academically under the tutelage of those six black woman, it never occurred to me until much later in my life, that my intellectual life was indelibly linked to the intellectual lives of black women. It wasn't until I became the graduate student of the woman I affectionately call "Mama Soul" that I fully understood.

Years before I ever met Masani Alexis DeVeaux, I read her articles in the black women's magazine *Essence*. At the beginning of my collegiate career *Essence* magazine was a crucial link to the black intellectual world, as it was for so many young women *and* men in the early 1980s. The magazine's focus on the lives of black women was an important counter to the re-emergent black nationalist movement of the 1980s that gave a regular forum, particularly on college campuses, to aging revolutionaries and upstart nationalists. My own political consciousness as a first-year college student in 1983 was largely formed sitting at the foot of one of these would-be nationalists, a former playa-playa, who after hearing a speech by Louis Farrakhan, devoted his life to the Nation of Islam, where he's been a minister for more than a decade. It was through Donald Smith, by then Donald Muhammad, that I was introduced to a slew of black thinkers including the poet Haki Madhubuti, historians Chancellor Williams, John Henrik Clarke, and Yosef

Ben-Jochannan, and of course standard-bearing black nationalists like Kwame Toure (Stokely Carmichael) and Farrakhan.
We rarely if ever discussed black woman thinkers except psychologist Frances Cress Welsing (bruh was a psychology major)
and Black Arts poet Sonia Sanchez. Even in the early stages of
the moment that I think of as the beginning of my intellectual
career, I could discern a gap between the knowledge that
Muhammad introduced me to (to give a brother credit, he did
make me a voracious reader) and the black women writers I
read in a magazine like *Essence.* The gap reflected the very
real tensions I felt between the black women on campus and
the largely male-centered leadership of the black student organization that Muhammad led and that I eventually succeeded
him in leading. Much of that tension came to a head, as it did
for much of Black America, in early 1986 with the release
of the film *The Color Purple*, Stephen Spielberg's cinematic
treatment of Alice Walker's Pulitzer-winning novel of the same
name.

For many folks of the post-Soul generation, the controversy
over the film *The Color Purple* was our indoctrination into
decades-old gender debates within the black community. And I
don't use the term indoctrination loosely: as young men and
women we were expected to choose sides. In short, many black
men felt that Walker's book, and particularly the film version of
The Color Purple, depicted black men in a way not quite befit-
ting the "Strong Black Men" we all thought we were. Even
more so, Walker was accused of colluding with the "white
man" in helping to further demonize the images of black men.
As television personality Tony Brown reflected at the time,
"I offer no excuses for the kinds of men that Walker wrote
about . . . but many of us who are male and black are too
healthy to pay to be abused by a white man's movie focusing on
our failures," adding that "it is a very dangerous film."[2] Brown's
comments of course beg the question, "Dangerous to whom?"
According to Leroy Clark, who was at the time a law professor

at Catholic University, "One of the most serious problems that the black middle class faces these days is image. . . . Blacks are thought to be good basketball players but the question remains can we be good physicists. Those image problems came from the reality that we were kept out of those activities but the image problem remains because of the way the media treats us."[3] There's no question that the mass media have colluded with the discourses of racism in America to create distorted and truncated images of black folk in this country, but the response of men like Brown, Clark, and those many black men *and* women who picketed the film's premiere in December of 1985 was directly correlated to the threat that the film, and by extension a black feminist critique, posed to the image and viability of the proverbial "Strong Black Man." Had the film's target not been the dominant patriarchal figure in the literary and cinematic worlds that Walker and Spielberg created, would the controversy over the film have been played out so publicly?

The debate over the lack of positive black male images in the work of black women artists actually began a few years earlier with the Broadway debut of Ntozake Shange's play *for colored girls who have considered suicide/when the rainbow is enuf* (1976) and Michele Wallace's *Black Macho and the Myth of the Superwoman* three years later. *for colored girls . . .* began as a series of poems that Shange and others presented in small clubs and coffeehouses in the San Francisco Bay area in 1974. With the help of her sister Ifa Iyam and Osborne "Oz" Scott, *for colored girls . . .* was transformed into a "choreopoem" and moved to New York City, where it eventually opened on Broadway at the Booth Theater in September of 1976. The play was structured around a series of vignettes performed by seven women, known as the "lady in brown," the "lady in yellow," the "lady in purple," the "lady in red," the "lady in green," the "lady in blue," and the "lady in orange," women who powerfully represented the diversity of black female identity if not a diversity of experience. As Sandra Hollin Flowers wrote in *Black American Literature Forum*, "Shange has given us an exquisite and very personal view of the politics of black womanhood and black male-female relationships," adding that the "truth is very painful as that depicted in *Colored Girls*, and in telling it one opens oneself up to charges of dividing the race and exposing blacks to ridicule by reinforcing stereotypes."[4]

Although many of the men portrayed in *for colored girls . . .* can be appropriately described as "mean/low-down/triflin/& no count,"[5] much of the criticism of Shange centered on the play's closing vignette which featured the "lady in red" telling the story of Crystal and Beau Willie Brown. Beau Willie is both verbally and physically abusive to Crystal and in the vignette's most critical moment, he tosses the couple's two young children out of the window of their fifth-floor apartment building, to their apparent deaths. Writing about Beau Willie more than fifteen years after the choreopoem first debuted on Broadway, literary scholar Neal A. Lester wrote, "This particular example of male brutality and Shange's general presentation of males throughout the play leave audience members seeing *for colored girls* as little more than another black feminist's ruthless and unjustified attack on all black men."[6] To add insult to injury (at least in the minds of some black folk) actress Trazana Beverley won a Tony Award for her portrayal of the "lady in red" in 1977.

Word of Michele Wallace's *Black Macho and the Myth of the Superwoman* surfaced weeks before its publication when *Ms.* magazine, the leading feminist magazine in the United States, excerpted portions of the book, and proclaimed that gender relations represented the core issue for Black America in the 1980s. The fact that Wallace's book was seemingly closely aligned to the mainstream feminist movement made it a difficult sell to many black folk, but ultimately it was the brash tenor of her criticisms of black men *and* women, that made her an easy target for those already uneasy about the work of Shange. More a black feminist manifesto than a scholarly study, Wallace examines black male–female relationships from the antebellum era through the civil rights movement. Tackling the myth of black female dominance during slavery Wallace writes, "The presumed dominance of the black women during slavery would not be quite enough to explain the full extent of black male anger, especially since it was more untrue than not. . . . Rather his actual gripe must be, at least in part, that the black women, his woman, was not *his* slave, that his right to expect her complete service and devotion was usurped."[7] Writing about the motivations behind the civil rights and Black Power movements, she asserts, "The motive was revenge. It was not equality that was primarily being pursued but a kind of superiority—black manhood, black macho—which would combine the ghetto cunning, cool, and unrestrained sexuality of black survival with the unchecked authority, control, and wealth of white power."[8] *Black Macho and the Myth of the Superwoman* is alternately funny, provocative, angry, and irreverent, and critical response to it was swift and affecting.

In an article mischievously titled "Aunt Jemima Don't Like Uncle Ben," noted curmudgeon Stanley Crouch wrote, "There is a backlash taking place in this country. Those whites within the media who felt betrayed or affronted by the anti-white, anti-[S]emitic and violent tendencies of black nationalism during the '60s are promoting a gaggle of black female writers who pay lip service to the woman's movement while supplying us with new stereotypes of black men and women. The celebration of the militant mediocrity and self-pity of Ntozake Shange and the horror stories of Gayle Jones . . . are part of that backlash," adding that "Michele Wallace's *Black Macho and the Myth of the Superwoman* is the latest in this series."[9] Even if Crouch's analysis were credible, he neglects the reality that some of those black nationalists may have given black women writers legitimate reasons to caricature black men. Trying to describe the position of black men who were critical of

Shange's play, Mel Watkins wrote in 1986 that "Their complaint, put simply, was that the play in its consistent and unwavering denigration of black men presented an unbalanced, simplified portrait that was consequently not only exaggerated and false but that also undermined the black man's struggle for acceptance in mainstream society."[10] Ahh, and there's the rub. In his essay "The Sexual Mountain and Black Women Writers" literary scholar Calvin C. Hernton was much less diplomatic in describing the motivation of black male critics of Shange, writing that "In a time when black men were striving for respect, here comes some middle-class, light-skinned bitch, putting black men down before the eyes of the white world."[11] Watkins and Hernton can be called out on trying to represent the views of all black men on Shange's play, but there's little doubt that they captured the sensibilities of the production's most vitriolic critics.

Perhaps missing in the analysis of those who were so critical of Shange and Wallace were the ways in which their writing affirmed the value of black women's lives in a society that often suggested that those lives weren't of value. In her book *Forty-Three Septembers*, Jewelle Gomez writes, "The inability to see ourselves as the center of anything, even our own lives, has in one sense allowed Black women to be the backbone of Black communities, but it has also limited our perspective on the world and that of our literary critics."[12] Gomez frankly states, "What was really infuriating to [Shange's] critics, however, was not that her poems libeled Black men (they did not) but that men were not central figures in them."[13] Writing in *Essence Magazine* in 1995, Gomez adds that "Shange's poems proclaimed the importance of Black women's voices to both our own survival and that of Black people. . . . I recognized not just the lives of my contemporaries but also those of my grandmother and great-grandmother."[14]

In the case of Wallace, there was a real emotional and psychic toll for her willingness to speak what was on her mind.

Though the legitimacy of some of her arguments were admittedly deserving of close scrutiny, the power of *Black Macho* remained in its ability to create a space for black women to speak openly to (and back to) black men on the subjects of sexism, misogyny, patriarchy, and violence against black women. In a 1983 interview, Wallace admitted to her sense of fear in the aftermath of the book's publication: "When people jump on you like that, especially when you're very young, you just clam up. You're like an animal behind caged bars. . . . I wasn't even necessarily aware of being afraid, but I could smell my own fear, so I had to admit it. I think of it now as a kind of death sweat—the kind of sweating that people must do before they die."[15] Wallace's comments are instructive, given the contriteness of her introduction to the Verso Classics edition of *Black Macho and the Myth of the Superwoman*, published in 1990. In a striking passage toward the end of her introduction Wallace writes, "When I first re-read the book in preparation for writing this, my immediate gut response was to destroy the book so that no one would ever read it again. . . . I wanted to destroy the book because my desire for something more from life than my marginal status as a black woman writer could ever afford was so palpable in its pages."[16] Though Wallace's comments are fully in sync with the opinions of so many writers about their first publications, it is also clear that they are the words of a woman who has been systematically "beat-up" and ostracized by those who were threatened by her analysis. As she reflected to interviewer Karen Boorstein, "I think possibly that it's a mistake to let men know that much about how you think. . . . Most people were not that willing to take the risk of telling the truth and I was, and I think that's a very dangerous foundation for a writing career."[17]

I was oblivious to the exploits of Michele Wallace and Ntozake Shange and the gender debates within the black community when the film *The Color Purple* was released in December of 1985, though in my first year of college a group of older black women students mounted a production of Shange's play, partially in response to the ruling black patriarchs on campus. For those of us who came of age listening to Run-DMC, Grand Master Flash and the Furious Five, Atlantic Starr, Teena Marie, Rick James, Glenn Jones, and Cheryl Lynn, the *Color Purple* debates were our first introduction to the gender crisis that engrossed so many segments of Black America. Behind closed doors (usually the executive board meetings of black student organizations), young black men like myself, who couldn't quite figure out what all the furor was about, were urged to close ranks against the "dirty little black feminists" who were threatening to destroy the sanctity of the Black Nation. A few years before Rush Limbaugh would derisively call feminists, "femi-nazis," the term "black feminist" (often followed by descriptive terms like "bull-dagger," "butches," and "black man emasculators") in many black circles was easily equated with terms like "KKK" and "white supremacy," and even more so because these were black women, who many believed were in collusion with white supremacists to "destroy" the "Black Man."

When black feminists were not being called bad names, they were surely being accused of being anti-intellectual. In their hugely problematic tome *The Endangered Black Family: Coping with the Unisexualization and Coming Extinction of the Black Race* (1984), Nathan and Julia Hare write (I'm citing from my autographed copy of the book signed February, 1985), "When you ask black feminists what is black feminism in the middle of some vigorous discourse, they suddenly fall silent and stammer, for they know no feminism other than that of the white feminism of the prime time news, the commercial magazines (for most don't even read alternative radical white feminist literature). Thus nobody has bothered to define black feminism, which seems strange and a shame, because white people surely will when it suits them if we don't."[18] The comments

of the Hares are not notable because of their blanket indictment of black feminists, but rather because of the apparent
utter ignorance of the couple about the already emergent body
of black feminist scholarship and criticism.

For example, *The Black Woman*, the groundbreaking
anthology edited by the late Toni Cade Bambara, was first
published in 1970. The now-classic *All the Women Are White,
All the Blacks Are Men, But Some of Us Are Brave*, edited by
Gloria T. Hull, Patricia Bell Scott, and Barbara Smith was published in 1982 and followed by the publication of the Barbara
Smith-edited *Home Girls: A Black Feminist Anthology* in 1983.
That same year the second edition of *This Bridge Called My
Back: Writings by Radical Women of Color*, edited by Gloria
Anzaldua and Cherrie Moraga was published. Audre Lorde's
nonfiction breakthrough, *Sister Outsider*, was published the
same year as the Hares' *The Endangered Black Family*,
although many of the book's essays had been previously published in other publications. *Ain't I A Woman: Black Women
and Feminism*, the first book by now well-known black feminist bell hooks, was published in 1981, by South End Press.
Nathan Hare was, in fact, part of the group of black women
and men writers and scholars that the journal *The Black
Scholar* brought together in 1979 to discuss "The Black Sexism
Debate." Lorde, June Jordan, Ntozake Shange, and Julianne
Malveaux were among the black feminists who logged in. In
this regard the Hares were disingenuous in their claim that
"nobody has bothered to define black feminism." I would sub-
mit that the Hares very consciously chose to ignore the emergent body of black feminist thought, because to acknowledge
that body of work was to acknowledge the legitimacy of a black
feminist movement, intellectual or otherwise. If the hip-hop
thug represents a threat to the sanctity of the image of the
"Strong Black Man," then the black feminist movement represents not just a threat to that image, but one capable of forcefully

asserting a critique of the sexism and misogyny practiced by the "Strong Black Man." For that reason the very legitimacy of black feminism had to be attacked and black feminist voices silenced within the black mainstream and demonized when heard in the white mainstream.

Birth of a Black Male Feminist

A few years ago I was invited to appear on *BET Tonight* to discuss black masculinity. In the hour-long pre-interview before I appeared on the show, I mentioned in passing to one of the producers that I considered myself a "male feminist." Unbeknownst to me while I was in the studio taping the segment, the producers decided to flash the phrase "male feminist" under my name whenever I appeared onscreen. I was made aware of this the next day when friends and family asked, rather pointedly, "What the hell is a male feminist?" Earlier in my life, had I been one of my friends and family members watching me on television that night, I too would have asked, "What the hell is a male feminist?" For some time now I've considered myself a feminist, so the decision of the BET producers to acknowledge me as such was not a problem. In fact I viewed my appearance on the network as a "feminist" as a unique opportunity to celebrate those of us who are serious about embracing politics that are anti-sexist/misogynist and anti-homophobic, those of us who are serious about uprooting impulses within the black community that work to deny community and diversity, in the best senses of the words. I obviously wasn't born a black male feminist. Those of us who dare claim the moniker are usually the product of a serious intervention by the women in our lives.

I had been in graduate school for less than a month when Anita Hill went public about the sexual harassment she endured while working for Clarence Thomas, who was being confirmed as the second black Supreme Court Justice in the fall of 1991. If the previous debates over the portrayal of black men were solely rooted in images that primarily existed on stage, in the pages of books and on movie screens, Hill's charges during the Thomas confirmation hearings had real-world implications. Consciously chosen by then-President George H. Bush, Thomas was essentially tagged to replace outgoing justice Thurgood Marshall as the high court's "black" vote. Despite Thomas's well-known conservative views, the Bush administration banked on the fact that his skin color—his fictive connection to an essential blackness—would disarm both liberal critics and traditional civil rights leaders. Thus within many black circles Anita Hill was viewed as the pawn of those within the Senate and others who would deny yet another black *man*, his opportunity to speak for the race.

Even Thomas understood the value of those fictive claims to blackness, depicting the confirmation hearings—a confirmation circus really—as little more than a "high-tech lynching," leading journalist Derrick Z. Jackson to quip that "If Thomas was lynched, no African American has ever been killed so softly."[19] Though I was unaware of it at the time the controversy perfectly illuminated the way that black male privilege functioned to silence black women. As UCLA law professor Devon Carbado writes, Hill "could not use her race to muster support from the Black community because Clarence Thomas, as a black man held the political ace . . . he had access to cultural and political narratives invoking the subordination of Black men that resonate politically with the Black community."[20] I admittedly followed the party line on this one, seeing the charges of sexually harassment as clearly an effort to defeat Thomas's nomination, particularly since large numbers of elite white men have rarely shown so much interest in sexual harassment against black women.

And thus came that first of several interventions that would dramatically alter my view of gender relations in the black community and elsewhere. If *Essence Magazine* primed me to at least hear the voices of black women (even if I didn't always take those voices seriously), it was in the classrooms of young white feminist scholars that I was forced to engage the work of mainstream and black feminists, work that challenged my initial view of the Clarence Thomas and Anita Hill dispute. It was in the classrooms of those young white feminists that I first read the groundbreaking essays of black feminist scholars Barbara Smith, Deborah E. McDowell, and the late Barbara Christian.[21] It was in the context of those classroom experiences that I picked up a copy of bell hooks's *Yearning: Race, Gender, and Cultural Politics*. I bought the book in a bookstore in Toronto and remember distinctly the feeling that I had just been party to some major transgression, contraband in the world of "Strong Black Men." In particular, hooks's essay "Representations: Feminism and Black Masculinity" introduced me to the concept of black male privilege, giving me some inkling of the way that I benefited from my position as a black man often at the expense of black women.

At the beginning of my graduate school career I was involved in various forms of campus activism (agitation really), particularly around the issues of increasing campus diversity and creating a more inclusionary curriculum. I was often disarmed when fellow black women activists often described my leadership style as sexist. I was generally respectful of black women and didn't trade in the kind of rhetoric that depicted black women as bitches and hos, so how could I be a sexist? It was hooks's essay that gave me the language to interrogate my actions in this regard: "Feeling as though they are constantly on edge, their lives always in jeopardy, many black men truly cannot understand that this condition of 'powerlessness' does not negate their capacity to assert power over black females in a way that is dominating and oppressive; nor does it justify and condone sexist behavior."[22] Reading the passage I understood that I often used my position as the "put upon" young black man to silence the ideas and concerns of my black women colleagues, particularly from my bully pulpit in the campus newspaper where I published a bi-weekly column. It also helped me to understand the ways that I unconsciously (I think) valued the opinions of other black men over those of black women, particularly because I was yet to understand the ways that gender and sexuality complicated what seemed like logical responses to racist acts in an often racist society. Over time I came to fully understand hooks's assertion that "Until black men can face the reality that sexism empowers them despite the impact of racism in their lives, it will be difficult to engage in meaningful dialogue about gender."[23]

Almost a year after I first picked up hooks's book I wrote my first "feminist" piece for the campus newspaper. In the essay "And God Created Woman" (after the Prince song of the same title), I owned up to the fact that most men are oblivious to the travails of women in American society and often embrace rudimentary forms of sexism naturally until they are challenged by women who are close to them. In the essay I acknowledged that charges of sexism "are often aimed at 'older, mature men' who should know better, but what event or person for that matter ever intervenes in the life of a male to point out the faultiness of his gender vision?"[24] The piece was really a tribute to those women who opened my eyes in this regard as I acknowledged the impact of my wife, my mother, Karen Mill-Courts and Jeanette McVicker, two white feminists I studied with, bell hooks, and a young black woman named Jiann Calhoun who was my biggest critic at the time. The essay marked the beginning of my career as a feminist critic, though it would be years still before the theories of black feminism were fully integrated into my personal life.

My transition from being a feminist on paper to one who was a feminist in practice began earnestly in the fall of 1993. I began my doctoral work in the Department of American Studies at the University of Buffalo that fall. I understood at the time the value of finding a strong supportive mentor to help shepherd me through the program. I sought out the advice of an older black woman, an advanced graduate student in the program, who suggested that I seek out Masani Alexis DeVeaux. I remember vividly her quip that even though DeVeaux was a feminist, she wasn't a "segregationist" and I admit that at the time I didn't quite know what she was talking about. A few weeks later when I walked into her classroom for the first time (five minutes late) for a class called "Red and Black Feminism"—a course focused on black and Native feminist writers—I perhaps got some inkling of what the woman was referring to as I realized that I was the only male enrolled in the class. To her credit, DeVeaux never treated my presence in her class as an anomaly; in fact she did much more, treating my presence as a radical opportunity to speak across gender, sexuality, generations, and ethnicity. Most important, she created an intellectual space to allow me the chance to "speak to" a wide range of black feminist writers, scholars, and artists. It was in that space that I first engaged Audre Lorde's book *Sister Outsider* and her essay "Uses of Erotic: The Erotic as Power;" it was in that space that I first came to love the work of Patricia Hill-Collins and her groundbreaking text *Black Feminist Thought: Knowledge, Consciousness and the Politics of Empowerment*; it was in that space that DeVeaux cultivated for me that I first broke bread with the words of Jewelle Gomez, whose collection of essays *Forty-Three Septembers* helped me make sense of the complicated web of blackness where gender, sexuality, sexual preference, class, and ethnicity intersected.

I still remember the night we discussed Lorde's "Uses of the Erotic: The Erotic as Power" in class as DeVeaux asked each of us to talk about the kinds of everyday activities that are erotic. I remember sheepishly sharing with the class—again a class of all women—the erotic pleasure of holding a freshly skinned kiwi-fruit in my hand (I kept to myself what I thought the cross-section of a strawberry looked like). What struck me powerfully about Lorde's essay was the notion that the "erotic has often been misnamed by men and used against women . . .

we have often turned away from the exploration and consideration of the erotic as a source of power and information, confusing it with its opposite, the pornographic."[25] The power that women could identify in the exploration of their own erotic pleasure was often siphoned off by men in their desire to objectify the sexuality of women. In other words, Lorde was making a distinction between the ability of women to find pleasure within themselves (not necessarily involving sex acts) and the desires of men to control women and their sexualities either by deriving pleasure in pornographic acts involving women or by deeming aspects of female sexuality "pornographic" and thus deserving of shame and derision, the feeling that sexual and erotic pleasures were somehow "dirty" and thus unavailable to "real" women.

This of course has had a dramatic impact within the black community as the "cult of respectability" has often deemed that it was necessary for black women to be sexually restrained and deny (at least publicly) any semblance of being sexual creatures. In this context it's easy to understand why black female entertainers like hip-hop artist Lil' Kim, R&B singer Tweet (who celebrated female self-pleasuring in the song "Oh My"), or actress Halle Berry, who took on highly sexualized roles in the films *Monster's Ball* (for which she won an Academy Award for best actress in 2002) and *Swordfish* (2001), are more intensely scrutinized within the black community, than say Berry's estranged husband Eric Benet, who was treated for "sex addiction" while married to her. What is really at stake is the inability of men, in this case black men, to give in to the impulses of the erotic (the ability of us to be *sensuously* healed) and cede the sense of control that comes from the "sexual conquering" (both real and imagined).

Lorde writes, "The erotic is a measure between the beginnings of our sense of self and the chaos of our strongest feelings. It is an internal sense of satisfaction to which, once we have experienced it, we know we can aspire . . . but giving in to the fear of feeling and working to capacity is a luxury only the unintentional can afford, and the unintentional are those who do not wish to guide their own destinies."[26] Throughout her essay Lorde posits the idea of the erotic that has little to do with sexual pleasure but rather defining the erotic in her life as "sharing deeply any pursuit with another person. The sharing of joy, whether physical, emotional, psychic or *intellectual* [my emphasis], forms a bridge between the sharers which can be the basis for understanding much of what is not shared between them, and lessens the threat of their difference."[27] Lorde's version of the erotic indeed became a metaphor for my own relationship with DeVeaux, our connection as black lesbian feminist poet and scholar and young black hip-hop intellectual and still-evolving feminist. Our relationship was not unlike the eroticism associated with mother and child: "Mama Soul" and her "Soul Baby." In another instance Lorde describes the erotic as "my capacity or joy . . . a reminder of my capacity for feeling. And that deep and irreplaceable knowledge of my capacity for joy comes to demand from all of my life that it be lived with the knowledge that such satisfaction is possible."[28] In this case Lorde's words help me to understand my choice to live a "life of the mind" as I found erotic pleasure in my work as a scholar and journalist, in the process locating the space where my love of knowledge and language and my sexuality (heterosexual desire) often intersected. What is instructive here is the ways that the words of a self-defined "black, lesbian, feminist, mother, poet warrior" offered an alternative vision for me to construct my masculine identity, one that was not beholden to dated tropes of black patriarchy. It was my first lesson in understanding how the work of black feminists, and later black gays and lesbians, could help affirm my sense of self as a black male heterosexual.

I first picked up Patricia Hill-Collins's *Black Feminist Thought: Knowledge, Consciousness, and the Politics of Empowerment* right after my first reading of hooks's *Yearning*.

I was turned off at first having become accustomed to hooks's "keep it real" style of black feminist speak. Trained as a sociologist, Hill-Collins's work was straightforward and at times dry, social scientist speak. Like so many folks who jump on the bandwagons of so-called progressive movements, I was perhaps caught up in the allure of hooks's celebrity, something I would also confront as I became more familiar with the work of some of hooks's more prominent black male colleagues. hooks made an engagement with feminism sexy, whereas the work of women like Patricia Hill-Collins or Stanlie James and Abena Busia forced me to deal with the critical intellectual questions that informed black feminist thought, questions that had little to do with my engagement with feminism and everything to do with the daily struggles of black women in a racist, sexist, and patriarchal society.[29] Those questions became clearer to me when I finally sat in a classroom with black and white women to discuss Hill-Collins's work. I suppose there was some aspect of my unconscious sense of masculine privilege that led me to believe that I could get "it"—meaning a black feminist perspective—on my own (perhaps also buying into the stereotype that I would get "screamed" on by a bunch of angry "feminazis"). And although it was easy to be lauded by my colleagues and mentors for my willingness to embrace black feminist writers on my own, truly "sitting at the feet" of these women (both metaphorically and physically) meant giving up on any sense of privilege (at least in those spaces) and allowing myself to embrace the sense of vulnerability that naturally comes with giving up privilege.

Hill-Collins's excavation of a black feminist intellectual tradition was critical to my own development as an intellectual because it forced me to broaden my concept of where intellectual production took place. According to Hill-Collins, "Reclaiming the Black Women's intellectual tradition involves examining the everyday ideas of black women not previously considered intellectuals," thus her claim that "Musicians, vocalists, poets, writers, and other artists constitute another group of Black women intellectuals who have aimed to interpret Black women's experiences" resonated with me in very powerful ways.[30] In retrospect, I have to admit that my work on "organic" or "Gramscian" intellectuals within the black popular music tradition was not solely informed by the work of black celebrity intellectuals like Cornel West and Michael Eric Dyson, but by the work of Patricia Hill-Collins. Thus, ironically, it was the work of this black feminist writer who influenced my view that black male artists like Marvin Gaye and R. Kelly (who both exhibited questionable and even criminal behavior toward women) were legitimate social critics or organic intellectuals.[31] This is not to suggest that I only found value in Hill-Collins's work when she broadened her perspective beyond black feminist thought. On the contrary, Hill-Collins's book has most profoundly influenced my ability to "read feminist;" in other words, to be able to identify a black feminist perspective in work I do as a scholar of popular culture and as a journalist.

In terms of my ability to "read feminist," Hill-Collins's description of the various "controlling images" that inform how American society perceives and ultimately deals with black women has been very influential. Hill-Collins identifies the "mammy," the "matriarch," the "welfare mother," and the "Jezebel" or "whore" as the most prominent of these controlling images, arguing that "As part of a generalized ideology of domination, these controlling images of Black womanhood take on special meaning because the authority to define these symbols is a major instrument of power . . . these controlling images are designed to make racism, sexism and poverty appear to be a natural, normal and an inevitable part of everyday life."[32] She argues that "Confronting the controlling images forwarded by institutions external to African-American communities should continue as a fundamental concern of Black feminist thought," but cautions that "this effort should not obscure the equally important issue of examining how African-American institutions also perpetuate notions of Black Women as the Other."[33] In this regard, Hill-Collins provides a blueprint to explicate, for instance, the complex web in which various images of black women exist in the videos of black male hip-hop artists. Not only do these young black men have an interest in "controlling" the images of women that appear in their videos, the largely white male elite owners of the popular culture industry derive wealth from the circulation of these often pornographic images of black women. The fact that these images are then used to inform public policy around domestic issues that adversely affect black and brown women—welfare reform, health care, aid to dependent children, childcare benefits, unemployment, underemployment, incarceration, etc.—further complicates what's at stake when black feminists such as Patricia Hill-Collins, Angela Davis, Joy James, Cathy Cohen, and others call for interventionist strategies among black feminist thinkers to address these conditions.

But it was really with the work of Jewelle Gomez that I felt as though I had a place in the feminist movement. Gomez's *Forty-Three Septembers* is a collection of personal essays about her family, friends, and fellow travelers, interspersed with critical pieces on playwright Lorraine Hansberry, black women's speculative fiction, the black protest tradition, and black lesbian literature. There's no doubt that Gomez's personal reflections on her mother, great-grandmother, and her father, Duke, were what drew me initially into the book. Gomez's *Forty-Three Septembers*, like Lorde's *Zami: A New Spelling of My Name*, helped humanize her to readers in a society that regularly dehumanizes those who choose identities seemingly out of sync with the mainstream, be it welfare mothers, the homeless, trenchcoat-wearing high-schoolers in the Midwest, or in this instance black lesbian feminists. In this regard, Gomez's book was the first feminist work that I read that spoke directly to me, directly addressing our common humanities, but also speaking to black men in a way that wasn't threatening and accusatory. This is not to say that I felt that the writings of other black feminists could be described as "threatening," but reading Gomez was like having a conversation on the stoop with an older sister or cousin that you might have had a boyhood crush on.

I felt as though I was sitting on that stoop, in particular, as I read Gomez's essay "Wink of an Eye." In the essay Gomez frames her relationship with her father as a metaphor for the positive relationships she had with men during her childhood and teen years. But she laments, "I'm not certain if it's simply my getting older or that the times are changing. As the years pass, it becomes harder to find Duke in male friends."[34] As she elaborates, "Each year the Black men I know express more bitterness, less hope. There are many valid reasons, of course. Much is made of manhood and the subtle and blatant ways that Black men are told they will never be good enough are stunning."[35] Although Gomez names two heterosexual black men who had been very supportive of her, particularly after she "came out" in the mid-1970s, she was able to find Duke in the "subtle gay winks of Black men, thrown past unsuspecting heterosexuals, letting me know there was a community."[36] She goes on to describe those black gay men as "comforting and familiar, like the expansive clink of my father's pocket change."[37] And it was the collapsing of her father's image—a large black man, married to two women—with that of those gay black men that particularly struck a chord in me. Gomez describes a dying Duke in the hospital keeping up a "flirtatious patter" with his male nurse, adding that "my father never acted like that made either of them less of a man. All that mattered was that he could still make connections with other people."[38]

When Gomez was with Duke, her few heterosexual black male friends, and the community of black gay men who embraced her, including the late poet Essex Hemphill, she envisioned a space where they could "revel in the feel of being brothers and sisters."[39] According to Gomez "There's a sensuous texture to Black life: the music, the use of words, the sensory pleasures of food, of dance. . . . The commonality of our past and the linking of our future make the bond sensual and passionate, even when it's not sexual."[40] And I must confess that it was in those classrooms with Alexis DeVeaux and so many of the other women in the room that I first experienced the sensuality of black life among women with whom I was not sexually involved. Not that such opportunities hadn't presented themselves in the past, but admittedly I was a young man who often gauged my relationships with black women on the basis of how physically attractive I found them. Although this is an aspect of my masculinity that I still struggle with, I've learned to enjoy the sensual possibilities of my relationships with black women—as intellectuals, as mentors, as colleagues, as friends, etc.—without reducing them to possible sexual conquest. It was only as I sat and truly listened to my black women partners in feminism, that I began to realize truly productive relationships with women other than my wife. Unlike portrayals of black feminists that depicted them as dangerously divisive to the black community and destructive to the concept of the "Strong Black Men," I found women who helped me realize a more powerful humanity in myself. I came to truly believe, as Barbara Ransby argues in her essay "Fear of a Black Feminist Planet," that "black feminism embodies a revolutionary potential, for both men and women. We see the need to redefine exploitive class relations, dismantle racial hierarchies and, at the same time, redefine what it means to be men, women and sexual beings."[41]

My Black Male Feminist Heroes

Like many young men in America, my initial sense of what feminists were was couched in popular descriptions of them as "man haters" and "bra-less lesbians." A child of the post–civil-rights era, I was among a generation of young blacks who actively consumed the politics and rhetoric of a distinct '80s-styled neo-black nationalism as embraced in the speeches of Louis Farrakhan and a host of other part-time theorists and full-time demagogues, who had convinced me to look skeptically and suspiciously at those black women who called themselves feminists. Finally it was Alexis DeVeaux who taught me the importance of being a black man who found value in closing ranks with those black women who continuously resisted and challenged the sexism, misogyny, and patriarchal norms found among black communities and institutions. Because of DeVeaux there were many quiet moments where I engaged the work of bell hooks, Michele Wallace, and Patricia Hill-Collins and still more quiet moments now where I find feminist grounding with the intellects of Joy James, Kimberle Crenshaw, and Sharon Patricia Holland—this next generation of black feminist scholars—whose books and articles are crucial components of the knowledge that I introduce to my students as a scholar of African-American culture. My experience is not unlike that of Gary L. Lemons who argues that a "new generation of young prowomanist Black men have emerged, many of whom have studied with some of the most well-known Black feminists of the day. We speak in womanist terms, calling for Black male accountability on the issue of sexism. . . . I am a self declared womanist feminist precisely because of the teaching and scholarship of Black women feminists."[42]

It was about a decade ago when I first came out of the closet and acknowledged to the world that I considered myself a feminist. Though it has often been much easier to represent feminist politics in my writings and teaching than in the field (where shit is real), I've never passed on the opportunity to confirm, as Manning Marable once described it, my "groundings with my sisters." Many black men who consider themselves feminist were initially influenced by black women feminists (keep in mind, not all black women consider themselves feminist, a measurement of the level of patriarchy's influence in some black spaces). But what was just as crucial to my own development, was the identification of other black men who embraced feminist politics. In his essay "'When and Where [We] Enter': In Search of a Feminist Forefather," Lemons identifies Frederick Douglas and in particular W.E.B. Du Bois as role models for generations of black male feminists who have emerged over the last century or so. I was not fortunate to have read the work of Lemons during the formative stages of my black feminist development, but I did find inspiration in the voices of other black male writers.

I was already deep in the throes of my meditations with Collins's *Black Feminist Thought* and hooks's *Yearning: Race, Gender and Cultural Politics* when I cracked open a copy of Greg Tate's *Flyboy in the Buttermilk* (1992). I was familiar with Tate's brilliant riffs on black music and culture in the pages of *The Village Voice* (which as a teenager I always viewed as that "gay paper"), but it was Tate's obituary for Miles Davis that awakened me to the existence of a black male feminism. In the essay, "Silence, Exile and Cunning: Miles Davis in Memoriam," Tate admits that Davis is the "black aesthetic. He doesn't just represent it, he defines it. . . . Miles rendered black a synonym for the best of everything," but takes Davis to task for his almost gleeful descriptions of his acts of violence against women in his autobiography *Miles* (1989).[43] Tate confesses that "Much as I loved Miles, I despised him after reading about those incidents. Not that I worshipped the ground he spit on, but because I'd loathe any muhfukuh who violated women the way he did," adding that "Miles may have swung like a champion, but on that score he went out like a roach." Tate's critique of Davis was likely inspired by Pearl Cleage, who the year before offered a retort to Davis's autobiography with the book *Mad at Miles*.

In his autobiography Davis admits to beating his wife, the actress Cicely Tyson, recounting how "one time we argued . . . and I just slapped the shit out of her." The attack was instigated by Davis, who was jealous of a male friend of Tyson's who often called their home. According to Davis, after Tyson encouraged her friend not to call again ("Miles don't want me talking to you anymore"), he "slapped her again. So she never did pull that shit again on me."[44] Pearl Cleage's book *Mad at Miles* was meant as a fiery retort to Davis's admission of violent abuse against his wife. According to Cleage, Davis was "guilty of self-confessed violent crimes against women such that we should break his albums, burn his tapes and scratch up his CD's until he acknowledges and apologizes and rethinks his position on The Woman Question."[45] Davis's status as resident black genius often discouraged the kind of scrutiny that Cleage and Tate were willing to offer. In that regard Tate's essay offered a template to deal with a spate of demonic black male geniuses—R. Kelly, Bill Withers, and Dr. Dre come immediately to mind.[46]

Although R. Kelly's indictment on over twenty charges of child pornography has been front-page news and Davis gleefully recalled his own transgressions, less known are rumors that Withers physically abused actress Denise Nicholas during their brief marriage in the early 1970s. Withers's low-key style of music (often referred to as "folk Soul") on tracks like "Lean on Me," "Grandma's Hands,"and "Lovely Day" seemed to betray the idea that he was capable of such violence (though his song "Who is He? (And What is He to You?)" suggests otherwise). Explaining why Davis was the primary target of her venom, Cleage admits that Davis was the "one who admitted to it. Almost bragged about it. . . . Nobody was ever able to show me where David Ruffin (the late lead singer of the Temptations) admitted to hitting Tammi Terrell in the head with a hammer," and "Nobody was able to provide me with a quote from Bill Withers describing how he beat up Denise Nicholas when their marriage was grinding to a painfully public close."[47] In contrast to Withers (and Ruffin), hip-hop producer extraordinaire

Dr. Dre could easily be implicated for the misogynistic tenor of his lyrics with the "gangsta rap" innovators N.W.A. (Niggas With Attitude) when he attacked rapper and talk show host Denise "Dee" Barnes in January of 1991.

Dr. Dre was upset that Barnes, as host of the hip-hop video program *Pump it Up!* allowed former N.W.A. member Ice Cube a forum to criticize the group. Dr. Dre confronted Barnes in a Los Angeles club and while his bodyguards held the crowd back, he proceeded to beat Barnes, at one point attempting to toss her down a flight of stairs and chasing her into a bathroom where he stomped on her hands.[48] Barnes later filed a $22 million suit that was eventually settled out of court.[49] Dr. Dre pleaded no contest to misdemeanor battery charges and was fined $2513 and sentenced to 240 hours of community service and ordered to pay $1000 to a victims' restitution fund and produce an anti-violence PSA.[50] Though Tim Dog used the attack against Barnes as a prop in his bicoastal "war" with N.W.A. ("NWA ain't shit to me/Dre beatin' on Dee from *Pump it Up!*" from "Fuck Compton"), there was very little public outcry from the hip-hop community. Recounting her efforts to organize black women feminists and hip-hop artists, scholar Tricia Rose notes that "One favored, but unrealized" response to the attack was to pressure prominent male hip-hop artists like Public Enemy lead Chuck D, "especially as it was claimed that he and others condemned the Dre's attacks in private conversations."[51] Unable to galvanize such figures, Rose laments that "In hip-hop, where loud and sustained responses reign, the silence following abuses of black women is deafening."[52] Echoing Rose's concerns, Cleage chided black feminist writers for not stepping up to speak out about the attack on Barnes, "because the noise of the world in which Dee Barnes lives and works—the world in which our teenage children go to school and fall in love and decide to have sex—is so insistently loud and irritating to our thirty- or forty-plus years that we tune it

out completely and hope it will just go away.">[53] She even face-
tiously asks what the response might have been if figures like
Ishmael Reed and Amiri Baraka had transformed their written
attacks against black feminists into real physical attacks.

   Both Cleage's and Tate's response to Miles Davis's autobiography and Dr. Dre's attack on Barnes occurred at a moment
when Shahrazad Ali's self-published *A Black Man's Guide to the
Black Woman* became an underground best-seller among black
readers. In the book Ali openly advocated the use of violence
against black women, a suggestion that gained credibility among
some in the black community because it was written by a black
woman. The book was roundly criticized by black journalists
and scholars like the late sociologist Vivian Gordon who edited
the book *Confusion by Any Other Name: Essays on the Negative Impact of the Blackman's Guide* (Third World Press, 1990)
and some black-owned bookstores refused to sell it. Essentially
published by Ali's vanity press, the book's initial $10 price tag
made it very attractive to those who might have shared Ali's
desire to "enlighten the black man and create a revolution of
positive change in black relationships."[54] One Washington, D.C.-
area bookstore reported that "We've been taking in $3,000 to
$4,000 each week retail for a month (roughly 300 book sales
weekly) . . . the same thing is happening all over the country."[55]
A year later the book clearly resonated in the thinking of
N.W.A. members MC Ren and Eazy-E who quipped "the bitch
deserved it" in response to Dr. Dre's attack on Denise "Dee"
Barnes.[56] To counter the popularity of Ali's book, Cleage's *Mad
at Miles: A Blackwoman's Guide to Truth* was published by her
own vanity press and was clearly intended (as the subtitle suggests) to confront the issue of violence against black women
directly with the kinds of readers that had supported Ali's *The
Blackman's Guide to Understanding the Black Woman.*

   With so many black men of my generation (I was 25 at the
time) unable to publicly discuss any hint of reservation about
physical attacks against black women, Greg Tate's criticisms of

Miles Davis had a powerful impact on me. Earlier in his career, Tate had also challenged Public Enemy for wanting to "reconvene the black power movement with hip-hop as the medium . . . as well as a revival of the old movement's less than humane tendencies" including misogyny and "gaybashing."[57] I was still a card-carrying junior black nationalist when Tate first published his review of Public Enemy's *It Takes a Nation of Millions to Hold Us Back* (required listening at the time) in 1988 and I remember thinking at the time that he was a "punk" and a "sell-out." A few years later I fully understood the importance of Tate's critique and the kind of bravery it entailed. Tate was the first black man who I publicly witnessed break ranks with patriarchy.

But Tate also used his Afro-Boho Niggeratti pulpit to share the stage with black women artists. In the essay "Cinematic Sisterhood," also collected in *Flyboy in the Buttermilk*, Tate gives love to the artistry of black women filmmakers Michelle Parkerson, Jackie Shearer, Daresha Kyi, Ellen Sumter, Dawn Suggs, Zeinabu Irene Davis, and Ayoka Chinzera. According to Tate, "The intention of this article is to move perception of black women from margin to center stage. . . . We need to take stock in those Black filmmakers, male, female, indifferent, who serve up visions of black life beyond homies slangin' and gang-bangin'."[58] The essay was written at a time when black male filmmakers such as Spike Lee, John Singleton, Matty Rich (*Straight Out of Brooklyn*), The Hudlin Brothers, and Robert Townsend (*The Five Heartbeats*) were being celebrated as the best hopes for the black cinematic tradition. Tate's critical intervention was even more valuable because of the very problematic portrayals of black women that were featured in the films of Lee and Singleton who were the most successful and celebrated of those black male filmmakers.[59]

In the book's closing essay "Love and the Enemy" Tate takes stock of the black community at large. His closing shot was indeed a provocative one: "If Black Male leadership doesn't move in the direction of recognizing the pain and trauma beneath the rage, as the work of Toni Morrison, Ntozake Shange, Alice Walker, bell hooks and other women writers have done . . . then what we're struggling for is merely the end of white supremacy—and not the salvaging of its victims."[60] I have a vivid memory of one reviewer who viewed Tate's pro-feminist stance in this instance, and others throughout the book, as an overt attempt to cater to female audiences. In other words he called him a punk and thus has been the critique offered by so many black men (and women) of black men who stand behind progressive gender politics.

In his critical observations on black culture, Greg Tate offered a vision of the role that black men can play in creating and sustaining a black feminist worldview. Literary scholar Michael Awkward went a step further with his seminal essay "A Black Man's Place in Feminist Criticism" which appears in his book *Negotiating Difference: Race, Gender, and the Politics of Positionality* (1995). The essay was largely a response to the kinds of resistance that Awkward faced from fellow feminist critics regarding his desire to "read" and write feminist. Awkward's first book *Inspiring Influences: Tradition, Revision, and Afro-American Women's Novels* (1989) provided such readings of black literature. Awkward is on the leading edge (both in age and scholarly acumen) of a generation of black male scholars for whom the study of feminist theory was a regular activity, thus his *scholarly* interest in black feminist theory is not surprising. Virtually all of the major black male public intellectuals— especially those on the Left—have made it their business to give some lip service to the politics of the black feminist movement. But the reality is that failure to do so would have a direct impact on everything from book sales and speaking engagements to these men's ability to hold endowed chairs at major universities and colleges. Awkward, though, has worked against that grain to openly acknowledge the contradictions of claiming a black male feminism, while remaining wholly invested in the importance of it. In *Negotiating Difference*, Awkward writes, "The most difficult task for a black male feminist is striking a workable balance between male self-inquiry/interest and an adequately feminist critique of patriarchy. To this point, especially in response to the commercial and critical success of contemporary Afro-American Women's literature, scores of black men have proved unsuccessful in this regard."[61] Ultimately Awkward sees the rewards of black feminism in its ability to help redefine "figurations of 'family matters' and black male sexuality."[62]

Awkward traces his own quest for a transformative black masculinity in his relationship with his alcoholic mother. In *Scenes of Instruction: A Memoir*, Awkward writes, "Loving my mother required that I try to understand why she drank, why she frequently neglected her children's needs . . . loving her meant recognizing logical connections between my father's brutality and her drinking." Awkward found common ground with his mother via her constant reminder that he not be like his father. According to Awkward, "Doing anything but pursuing black feminist insights would have meant being like my father. I could no more have rejected feminism than I could have chosen not to love my mother."[63] But Awkward is conscious that he also could be perceived as an opportunist, adding that "To speak extensively about why I am a black male feminist is to expose myself to charges that I have visited upon my mother a discursive violence similar in intensity to the unimaginable physical pain she suffered at my father's hands."[64]

Such concerns are often voiced by black feminists, who while supportive of the emergence of black male feminists, are cautious about their motivations and intents. In her essay "Negative Images: Towards a Black Feminist Creativity," Michele Wallace expresses ambivalence over Henry Louis Gates's editorship of the first *Norton Anthology of Afro-American Literature* and various literary series. Wallace asserts that Gates is "singlehandedly reshaping, codifying and consolidating the entire field of Afro-American Studies, including black feminist studies." She admits that Gates may be "well intentioned in his efforts to recognize and acknowledge the contributions of black women writers," but she laments he "demonstrates an ability to define black feminist inquiry for the dominant discourse in a manner as yet unavailable to black female critics. The results . . . are inevitably patriarchal." Finally she notes, "Having established himself as the father of Afro-American Literary Studies . . . he now proposes to become the phallic mother of a newly depoliticized, mainstreamed and commodified black feminist literary criticism."[65] Wallace's critique is echoed in the work of Joy James who argues that men "define the social and intellectual parameters of gender politics through literary nonfiction. Male writers who highlight the significance of female contributions can nevertheless engage in an *opportunistic* feminism [my emphasis]."[66] For example, Gates' recent acquisition of Hannah Craft's *The Bondwoman's Narrative* and subsequent sale of the 145-year-old slave novel to Warner Books might be interpreted as such opportunism.[67]

Many emerging black male feminists are even more conscious of the way patriarchal privilege affects even work intended to buttress the scholarship and activism of black feminists. For example, in his essay "Love Jones: A Black Male Feminist Critique of Chester Himes's *If He Hollers Let Him Go*," David Ikard asserts that "If black male critics are to be useful and productive to the black feminist project . . . they must stop policing black male borders and take the lion's share of the burden of redressing phallocentric readings of black male authored texts." He adds, "Before black men can productively engage black feminists on the issue of black masculinity, however, they must accept that their victimization in America as black men does not exempt them from participation in patriarchy."[68] As Ikard's comments attest, a real challenge exists for black male feminists in consciously policing their own patriarchal privilege even as they challenge the conventions of patriarchy, particularly when doing so in the name of black women. As I've suggested and Awkward and Ikard have co-signed, the real value of feminism to black men comes from its ability to literally transform our worldview, particularly in response to our acceptance of very rigid versions of black masculinity. In some regards, as scholars, whose ideas are often limited to the spaces of the classroom and books and journals largely read by our peers and graduate students, we work in relative "safety." Members of The Nation of Islam, for example, will unlikely set up a reading group to discuss *NewBlackMan*. Thus it is much more difficult for black men to own up to their backward-ass gender politics, in public—in the full view of the "community"—but this is the stance that longtime writer and journalist Kevin Powell took in his brilliantly brave essay "The Sexist in Me."

Originally published in the September, 1992 issue of *Essence* magazine, Powell's piece admits to an act of violence against one of his former girlfriends. In the essay Powell recalls, "I grabbed her by the seat of her shorts and pulled her back into the apartment. We struggled in the kitchen, the dining area and the bathroom. As we were moving toward the living room, I shoved her into the bathroom door. Her face bruised, she began to cry uncontrollably, and I tried to calm her down as we wrestled on the living room floor . . . shaking with fear and exhaustion, I watched my girlfriend run barefoot out of the apartment into the street." Writing about the incident a year later Powell admits that he "managed to join the swelling ranks of abusive men with relative ease," adding that "it wasn't until I committed a violent act that it hit me how deeply I believed women to be inferior to men."[69] In the essay Powell exhibits the kind of self-critical reflection that is absolutely necessary for the realization of a black male feminism.

At the time that "The Sexist in Me" was published, Powell was at the height of his mainstream popularity (if you consider being consistently portrayed as the "angry black man" on the very first season of *The Real World* as evidence of mainstream appeal), thus his self-critique carried a power that it wouldn't have coming from someone with less celebrity. Powell was also recognized as one of *the* critical voices of the hip-hop genera-tion, thus his commentary was in striking opposition to the status quo within the hip-hop nation, which couldn't even bring itself to hold Dr. Dre accountable when he attacked Dee Barnes. In his memoirs *Keepin' It Real: Post-MTV Reflections on Race, Sex, and Politics* (1997) Powell recalls some of the letters he received in response to "The Sexist in Me," including one brother who asked, "Man, why you gotta put your shit out there like that?" and another who wrote, "I bet you getting' a lotta pussy now, right?"[70] Both comments speak to the way that Powell was put into the unenviable position of being viewed as either an opportunist or a punk. According to Powell, "I'm no hero, nor was I trying to make myself out to be martyr or a sac-rificial lamb. . . . I simply wanted to tell the truth because I felt it was the only way I could ever begin to move forward."[71]

In the decade or more since Powell's unfortunate experi-ence with his girlfriend, he has been a very vocal and visible proponent of the need for black men to re-evaluate their rela-tionship with black feminism *and* their own masculinity. For example he has been a tireless supporter and advocate of the work of Aishah Shahidah Simmons, a black lesbian filmmaker who is completing a documentary called *NO!* which addresses the sexual abuse and rape of black women at the hands of black men. His commitment to challenging misogyny was powerfully articulated in his essay "Confessions of a Recovering Misogy-nist," which was initially published in the pages of *Ms. Maga-zine*. In the essay Powell admits, "Like a recovering alcoholic or a crack fiend who has righted his or her ways, I am merely cognizant of the fact that I have had some serious problems in my life with and in regard to women. I am also aware that I can lapse at any time."[72] Telling in the piece is Powell's explo-ration of past relationships with his mother and female col-leagues as he finds that he wasn't just a sexist, but harbored a real "hatred" of women, hence his referencing of himself as a recovering misogynist. One of the ways that Powell tries to remain grounded is by regularly challenging other black men regarding their sexist and misogynist attitudes. According to Powell, "Some men, young and old alike, simply cannot deal with it. . . . I truly wonder how many men actually listen to the concerns of women."[73]

Powell's support of black feminists and challenging of his own misogyny has also led him to question his homophobia. In his book *Who's Gonna Take the Weight? Manhood, Race and Power in America*, Powell reflects on a period in his adult life when he was struggling with alcoholism, his anger, and diminishing professional prospects. At that time he rented an apartment from an older gay man and he admits, "I had been guilty of verbally bashing, privately and publicly, men with his sexual orientation as 'fags' or 'homos'," but "this man, this gay Black man, taught me more lessons about manhood than one would think possible. . . . The source of his power—and he was powerful—was in his own simple humanity."[74] In many regards Powell's "moment of clarity" is a natural progression, because in so many ways homophobia is rooted in a hatred of women; if women are feared and hated for being women, gay men face the same for being thought of as *like* women (a dichotomous world where some heterosexual men define sexuality as who penetrates and who gets penetrated). If the hip-hop thug threatens the image of the "Strong Black Man" and the black feminist is capable of "speaking back to" the "Strong Black Man" then the black gay man is often viewed as a powerful reminder of what could happen to the "Strong Black Man" when white supremacy strips him of his masculinity. The black male homosexual is perceived as the very antithesis of the "Strong Black Male." But like black feminism, black gay men offer possibilities for all black men to rethink their own masculinities and sexualities in order to create more productive relationships within the black community.

Chapter 3

queers in a barrel

Man, the women's movement is ruling the world. It's turning our sons into faggots and our men into punks.

> quoted in Essex Hemphill's "In an Afternoon Light."[1]

Where oh where are all the real men?

> KRS-One "Ya Strugglin'"[2]

So an invitation came for me to address the masses during the annual Black Solidarity Day rally on campus. Black Solidarity Day is a day set aside annually on the first Monday in November. On that day black students on many campuses across the United States attempt to show unity with each other by sponsoring cultural events, wearing all-black outfits, singing the "Negro National Anthem" (James Weldon Johnson's "Lift Every Voice" which *nobody* seems to know the second verse to) and raising

Black Power fists. I was a fervent supporter of such events when I was an undergraduate (nothing like hordes of black students in black scaring the shit out of white folks), so I understood the spirit of the invitation. But I was also distressed by the invite, not simply because it was last minute, but because I wasn't the kind of brotha they really wanted to hear from on that day. I simply can't be one of them "kumbaya-we-are-the-descendants-of-Kings-and-Queens-uplift the race" kind of negroes anymore. If I have to sit through another Afro-Nubian fashion show concocted by nineteen- and twenty-year-olds who've just discovered their blackness and a few passages from the triumvirate of Malcolm, Karenga, and KRS-One, I might have to give up my ghetto pass.

It's a distress I regularly face in the classroom as many of my black students (and quite a few white ones) share this ongoing illusion that somehow everything in the black community (and America for that matter) will be all right if we can just pretend to be unified. It's bullshit to me, which is why I've always preached to my students that in the "field," where political struggle is real, "unity is myth and solidarity is strategy." It's not as if some of them high-falutin' middle-class civil rights Negroes *really* wanted to break bread with the likes of a Fannie Lou Hamer, Amzie and Ruth Moore, domestics, tenant farmers, and factory workers, but understood that folks like Hamer and the Moores were the kind of "niggas" you needed on the front line if you at war.[3] But a brotha is always up for a challenge, especially when amongst the folk, so I accepted the invite. I decided that if I was going to be given a pulpit that day in the church of "keeping it real" blackness, why not use it that day to talk about how real unity among black folk ain't gonna happen unless we put our homophobia and sexism in check. So I took a collection of "Strong Black Men" to task for their misogyny, homophobia, and other exploitive behaviors. Collectively, the crowd responded with an unspoken—though not silent—"What's this shit got to do with black solidarity?" As folks began to grumble amongst themselves it was clear that my young brothers and sisters, some of whom were my students at the time, weren't quite feeling a brotha on that day. Some folks storm out when I'm done and I overhear others saying, "I ain't come here to hear this shit." One of my favorite students even reported back to me some of the conversation she heard about my lecture on the bus. Still others, brothers floating between the "out low" and the "down low" come over to embrace and give thanks for "representin'" *all* the folks. I was never quite sure if some of the negative reaction was due to my critical stance around the issue of homophobia and sexism within black communities or whether there were real reservations about whether black gays, for example, were in fact members of the black community at all.

Some of the attitudes of my black students mirror the "don't ask, don't tell" policy the armed forces took in the early 1990s in response to the possibility that there were more than a few gays and lesbians among its ranks. As Ronald Simmons writes, "In the African American community, 'homophobia' is not so much a fear of 'homosexuals' but a fear that homosexuality will become pervasive in the community."[4] I would add that even the possibility that homosexuality may be perceived as pervasive in the black community by whites and others informs quite a bit of homophobia in the black community. The conventional thinking in this matter is perhaps best represented with the song "Not Natural" in which gospel artists Angie and Debbie Winans argue that homosexuality is "not natural" in the eyes of "God" and ultimately unnatural to black folk. To many of the black students in the audience that day I was airing the proverbial "dirty laundry" (and of course damaging the image of the "Strong Black Man"). For example, one young sister even queried me later via e-mail as to why I felt the need to *always* mention that Langston Hughes and Countee Cullen may have been homosexuals. In her mind I was disrespecting them by mentioning their homosexuality. At one point she even baited me: "Professor Neal, would you want to be known as a great professor who teaches black studies or that *Gay* professor?"

In an era when R. Kelly's child "sexcapades" dominate black ghetto tabloids, online chat rooms, and black-themed web-sites, I would probably get more respect from some of my stu-dents (and this includes some of the female students) for being rumored as sexually harassing one of my female students, than being suspected of being gay. And I'm conflicted when some of the rumors start to fly around about my sexuality, as if a black man can't affirm and defend the presence of gays and lesbians in our communities unless he's gay himself. In her essay "Living at the Crossroads: Explorations in Race, Nationality, Sexuality and Gender," the late scholar Rhonda M. Williams discussed the ambivalence she felt when she decided to "come out" in a campus newspaper at the University of Maryland, because she suspected that many of her students harbored feelings about homosexuality that were clearly homophobic. According to Williams her students were "uncomfortable voicing such views in the classroom (in my presence?), but would speak their minds to one another."[6] Williams's experience is not unlike that of many gay and lesbian black professors who feel obligated to "perform" identity for various campus constituencies. In his autobiographical performance piece *Strange Fruit: A Perfor-mance about Identity Politics*, scholar E. Patrick Johnson reflects on the time he spent as a faculty member at Amherst College. According to Johnson, "Amherst brought to the fore all of the 'Whatness' of my identity: blackness, queerness, maleness, lower classness, southerness, and so on. The pressure proved to be too much . . . the performance was spinning out of control. Then the material reality of it all set in and I became the object of emotional and psychological abuse—from colleagues and students."[7]

Although I'll never fully understand the realities of my lesbian and gay colleagues, I have shared some of their ambivalence over "coming out" to students because of the subtle ways that black heterosexual academics and intellectuals, particularly black men, are "already" queered in the eyes of our students and the black community at large. In his book *Are We Not Men?: Masculine Anxiety and the Problem of African-American Identity*, Phillip Brian Harper notes that within "some African-American communities the 'professional' or 'intellectual' black male inevitably endangers his status both as black and as male whenever he evidences a facility with Received Standard English—a facility upon which his very identity as a professional or an intellectual in the larger society is founded in the first place."[8] The fact that I engage in forms of writing and teaching that raise questions about the rigidity of heterosexual black male identity and affirm pro-feminist and anti-homophobic perspectives further "queers" my identity in the eyes of some of my students.

I've long realized that if I protest too much and openly admit to my students that I *am* a heterosexual, that it makes me as homophobic as they are, because I would largely be motivated out of the fear that they would think that I *was* gay. I suspect that the various anecdotes that I share with my students about my daughters are the way that I subconsciously—probably more conscious and deliberate than I want to admit—compensate for the possibility that some of my students will still see me as gay. I am all too conscious that my students, as Williams described it, "have come of age in a political culture that regularly recycles two signs of black dysfunction: antisocial black (male) criminality and (female) sexuality are the behavioral manifestations of contemporary black cultural chaos," so I fully understand their decidedly less than progressive gender and sexual politics, not unlike mine at the same age.[9] Political scientist Cathy J. Cohen reminds folk in her book *The Boundaries of Blackness: AIDs and the Breakdown of Black Politics* that "sexuality, or what has been defined by the dominant society as the abnormal sexuality of both black men and women (e.g., images such as oversexed black men in search of white women, promiscuous black women, and illegitimate baby producers), has been used to justify the implementation of marginalizing systems ranging from slavery to most recently workfare."[10] Thus in many of the worldviews of the hip-hop generation, gays, lesbians, and feminists may be as deviant as the hardcore criminal and the "chickenhead" and welfare mother. I have often joked with colleagues and friends that whenever I ask who the "feminists" are in my class, it's always five white women (all wearing jeans and open-toe sandals) and me with our hands up.

Feminism and anti-homophobic politics ain't exactly on the minds of my black students who often want their blackness affirmed and celebrated, not scrutinized and interrogated in the context of the "black studies" classes that they often view as a safe haven from white supremacy. And the field of black studies itself seems invested in maintaining the classroom as a space for the reproduction of normative black sexual and gender relations. Sharon Patricia Holland writes that "Although it is true that to some extent African American Studies has paid attention to feminism, it is abundantly clear that there is no room in the closet for discussions of sexuality that move beyond a heterosexist paradigm."[11] For example, a few years ago after a spirited discussion in my class about the importance of Bayard Rustin and Ella Baker to the civil rights movement, two of my female students followed me back to my office to get some clarification as to the reasons why Rustin was jettisoned from the mainstream leadership of the movement. As I explained that it surely had something to do with Rustin's radical past as a political organizer, it also had a lot to do with the fact that Rustin was openly gay within a movement whose leadership was significantly drawn from black male clergy whose views on homosexuality were at best barely tolerant and at worst openly antagonistic. As I explained this to these young women, one of my older male colleagues, who was eavesdropping on the conversation, came from clear across the room to interject that Rustin's sexuality had nothing to do with his leaving the movement but the fact that he wanted to "return to New York to do work." It was clear to me that his intervention had less to do with denying the homophobia of the movement's male leadership and had everything to do with denying that Rustin was even gay.[12]

The semester in which I gave the Black Solidarity Day speech I taught a class called "Interrogating Blackness," the first class that I taught in which I purposely pushed against the boundaries of "acceptable" black identities. I initially wanted to call the class "Queering Blackness"—a class that sought to examine how *certain* black bodies are "queered" or made to seem "strange" and "unusual" in the context of very conservative notions of black identity—but knew that such a course title would drive away students who only think of queerness in relation to homosexuality. And although we were going to read at least one text by an out lesbian author, most of the texts dealt with the traditional meaning of "queer" in relation to blackness. My intent was to challenge students, particularly the black students in my orbit, to think seriously about the diversity that exists within blackness, especially around the themes of gender and sexuality. As such I deliberately tried to provoke them on the first day of class via the course syllabus that contained a short piece of fiction in which I imagined how that first class session might proceed.

Course Description (The Big-Daddy Boogie Down-Remix)

Interrogate blackness? Yo, what the fuck that mean, kid? I ain't tryin' to integrate shit. (That's interrogate, bruh.) I'm trying to be straight up black in this bitch. (And what exactly is black?) You know black . . . hardcore, ghetto-ass black—black like that nigga Jigga. Uknowwhaimsayin'. I know you gonna keep it real in this bitch right? (So what you sayin'? Folks gotta come up from the 'hood to really understand blackness?) Naw, I ain't sayin' all-a-that, but you know, what a busta know about keepin' it real? Livin' up in the burbs and shit. (So folks who are takin' care of fam and trying to do for their peeps by living in the right school districts without hassling wit fools tryin' to gank them on the regla aren't really keepin' it real?) There a nigga go puttin' words in my mouf . . . (So what you sayin', a middle-class nigga like myself is a sell-out?) Naw fuck that, what I wanna know is what that quote from this Mfer Kendall Thomas is about wit' that shit about gays and lesbos? What that shit got to do wit being black? That shit supposed to be in one of dem queer studies classes. (So you sayin' gay people ain't really black?) There this nigga go again…all I'm sayin' is you gotta choose, black folks ain't got no time to be fightin' AIDS and shit like that. I'm just strugglin' just wit' my own black ass tryin' to be just black. Naw on the real, I'm wit' Ice Cube on this one"true niggas ain't fags." (So what'chu sayin' is that Audre Lorde, Langston Hughes, Countee Cullen, Alain Locke) Who dem niggas? (James Baldwin, Essex Hemphill, Bessie Smith . . .) Naw, really who dem niggas? (Well the late Audre Lorde was an internationally known lesbian, warrior, poet, feminist, anti-racist activist) Feminist? We ain't readin' no feminist shit in this class are we? (Well bell hooks is a feminist. So is Michael Awkward.) Ain't no brotha supposed to be no damn feminist, unless he gay or a punk ass. (I consider myself a male feminist.) Yo kid this nigga crazy. How you gonna be teaching about black people wit' all this other shit on the table. Man, black is black, and if it ain't about respectin' the black man, the original man, it ain't black. (Oh so that's where we at? Aight Cool. . . .)

My intent was not to antagonize my students, but admittedly the description was a compilation of many exchanges that I have had with students during my career over issues of gender and sexuality and I wanted to make clear what kind of issues we were dealing with in the context of the class. And perhaps I too could be faulted for my linguistic caricaturing of the hip-hop generation male as antithetical to the very idea of community that I was trying to champion in the class.

My concerns were not without merit. Case in point, when the class was finally scheduled to read and discuss Jewell Gomez's collection of short stories *Don't Explain*—the book's title drawn from a short story which describes the centrality of Billie Holiday's music to the lives of a group of black lesbians in the 1950s, I swear that half of the students in a class of fifty students disappeared the two weeks that were devoted to reading and discussing the collection. Got all this rhythm from some of the most outspoken of the students about the book containing too much graphic sex (meaning the stories where two women kiss and caress each other and one of them has an orgasm). Such concerns didn't seem to faze them in some of the other pieces of fiction that we read in the class that contained graphic heterosexual sex. As Ron Simmons suggests, heterosexism, "the belief that heterosexual sex is good and proper and homosexual sex is bad and immoral," grounds a fair amount of the homophobia that finds acceptance in black communities and institutions, particularly when buttressed by religious doctrine.[13] In addition, as activist Tracy Jones notes, there is a general belief that there is a hierarchy of "sins" within the Black Church such that homosexuality was not just wrong, "but more wrong than any of the other sins. More unforgivable than any other acts of immorality, like adultery."[14]

When my class fell into group therapy mode one day after one white student (there were seven white students in the class) accused another white student of anti-Semitism (this mind you in a class that supposedly interrogates *Blackness*), it struck me that for some of my students (who expressed their homophobia with an ease usually reserved for wiping one's ass after a shit), a public expression of anti-Semitism was a clear social and political faux pas (a punishable sin really), but homophobic rage didn't even deserve to be acknowledged, let alone challenged. In this case, the free-flowing homophobia of the students in the class was also aided by the fact that they couldn't visually identify students in the class who might have been lesbian or gay (though there were a few in the class), so they felt as though their honesty would be unfettered. For example, even though some of my black students feel as though black studies classes are their own sacred spaces and that white students in these classes are encroaching, the "whiteness" of their peers makes them visible in a way that few black students would openly challenge their presence in the class. But "queerness" is only visible to them in the most superficial and caricatured of forms, and when such forms are not visibly present (I'm talking about the "faggotized" black man or Snap Queen and butch-femme), some students feel free to relish their homophobia and queer bashing.

This was made painfully clear a few years earlier when David, my gay graduate assistant, was forced to "come out" in class. David had heard comments like "you can't be real black man and be gay" one time too many and decided to make his queer-ness visible as a means of challenging the student's homophobia and stereotypical opinions about homosexual identities. It was a particularly brave and risky endeavor on his part and I initially had reservations about him coming out in class, because of the ways black bodies, in the context of the classroom, have histor-ically been used as information repositories of all that ails black America. So many of us who have come of age in the post–civil-rights era and attended white institutions of higher learn-ing have memories of the times that we, as the one or two black students in a class, were asked to describe what living on wel-fare was like, as if somehow that was a fundamental part of our communal identities. But David saw his coming out as a "teaching moment" and on those grounds he proceeded. Of course most of the students were shocked (simply shocked!) that he was gay because "he didn't look gay." Understandably their homophobia quickly settled underground when they came to terms with the fact that the *gay* teaching assistant (as he came to be known) was the one charged with grading their papers.

David and a few of the black gay men who have been in my classes in the past were in the house when I spoke at that Black Solidarity Day rally on campus. Virtually every one of them came up to me and gave me a "black man pound" in thanks for my acknowledgment of their presence in a room in which many desired that they remain invisible, if not totally disconnected from our mythical black community. My relationships with these men were premised on the fact that I always viewed the classroom as a safe haven for what I view as the performance of a progressive black masculinity. It is perhaps because of my comfort zone in the classroom that my comments at the Black Solidarity Day gathering have resonated so powerfully within me. If I was cognizant of being "queered" in the eyes of my students, what are the implications for a heterosexual black man to challenge homophobia in the light of day, in the street and on the corner as Essex Hemphill described it in his short essay "In an Afternoon Light."

I remember a brother, getting straight clowned in the barbershop one day. I was already sitting in the barber's chair when he came in with his boom-box in tow, listening to what could only be described as "Paradise Garage" classics.[15] Whether he was gay or not was beyond the point, because for many of the men in the shop his choice of music and decidedly "feminine" sensibilities marked him as "queer." He barely turned down the music playing on his boom-box as he asked whether he could get a haircut on credit. He didn't seem to notice the big sign on the mirror behind us that said "no credit" and as such my barber dutifully denied his request and the brother turned around and left the shop. Black-owned barbershops, like black-owned beauty salons, represent gendered spaces in the black community. Where black-owned beauty salons are often the space where black women "speak back to" the accepted gender politics of the black community, black-owned barbershops are often less a space of personal disclosure and more so a space where black men continue to perform very rigid notions of black masculinity around acceptable topics of discussion such as politics, sports, music, and of course sex. Most black barbershops are in stark contrast to those in the city of Seattle, for instance, who are participants in the Down Low Barbershop Program, which uses barbershops to educate black men and others about safe sex. I was particularly cognizant of the conservative nature of black barbershops when my barber quipped, in response to the "gay" brother that just left his shop, "Don't bring that shit in here." I wasn't quite sure whether he was referring to the music, the request for credit, or his perceived sexuality. What I was quite sure of was that I was not gonna challenge *anybody* in the shop that day on their homophobia, especially not the cat using the clippers on my hair. Even as I write about that experience now, I know the real challenge was to confront the homophobia in the shop that day. I punked out when it really mattered.

Writing about being a "black male feminist" and espousing anti-homophobic politics in my courses is the easy part, actually challenging sexism or homophobia when I'm up in the barbershop or some other black institution is a whole different story. It was the same way when I had to confront my father's homophobia. My father, whose own embodiment of the "Strong Black Man" was a powerful influence on me in my drive to black manhood as a teenager, is the victim of a debilitating muscular disease. Once an active and vibrant man, the disease has left him unable to use his lower body and one of his arms. Unable to walk, he is essentially relegated to his rocking chair and bed. When he first showed signs of the disease and was still mobile to a certain extent my mother was able to help him around the house, though it became increasing clear that he would need a home-care worker. Most of these workers were women, but as his condition worsened, it became necessary for him to have stronger male assistants. I can still remember my mother's phone call: "Your father doesn't want a male nurse, because he thinks that they are all 'faggots.' Can you talk to him?" Talk to him about what? Here I was confronted with a clear case of homophobia, made even more absurd by the fact that my father's welfare could be adversely affected by his own homophobic views. My father did eventually agree to have a male nurse (a middle-aged brother who made it clear to my father that he was married and with children) although it was not because of any pressure that I put on him. In a world where black fathers and sons rarely bond over things that aren't explicitly masculine—baseball and male gospel quartets in the case of my dad and I—I was *paralyzed intellectually* in trying to offer an anti-homophobic response to the homophobia that threatened to *literally paralyze* my father.

The experience with my father was again a powerful reminder that the "NewBlackMan" politics that I embrace so comfortably and with such conviction in my writings and in my classroom, really exist in a separate universe from the "real world" in which I live. When I am profiled by law enforcement officers or women (usually white) clutch their purses in the corner opposite me in the elevator, their immediate thought is never to consider my feminist and anti-homophobic politics. Perhaps it is a measurement of my own homophobia that I am unwilling to break ranks with black masculine privilege, as it is expressed in my everyday life, choosing to do so in the safety of the classroom and my books and articles. But there are very serious real-world implications to the homophobia that circulates in black communities and institutions that demand that those of us who do embrace progressive views on black sexuality speak and act more forcefully in the face of these challenges.

Brothers on the DL and "Queers" at the Altar

On the evening of November 3, 2002 Gregory Love, an undergraduate student at Morehouse College, an all-male school located in Atlanta, Georgia, returned to his dormitory to take a shower. As he entered the shower area, Love, who was without his glasses, peeked into one of the stalls thinking that it was his roommate and, realizing that it wasn't, he stepped into the next stall. Aaron Price was in the stall that Love accidentally peeked into. Affronted by what he perceived as a homosexual come-on,

Price left the bathroom and returned a few minutes later with
the baseball bat that he used to beat Love, fracturing his skull
in the process. Love was likely targeted by Price because the
former was a member of the Morehouse Glee Club, which is
perceived by some students on campus as a repository for homosexuals. While recovering from his attack, Love was visited by
an undergraduate from Morehouse's sister school Spelman, who
informed him that gay and lesbian students from both institutions were staging a demonstration on his behalf. According
to Erin Edwards, Love responded that "He didn't believe the
crime was committed because he was a homosexual because
he doesn't see himself as homosexual."[16] I highlight Love's
response not because I believe he was likely in denial about
how his sexuality might be perceived by others, but because the
attack on him speaks volumes about the dangers associated with
even being perceived as a homosexual among groups of people
who feel that violence is an acceptable way to express their
hatred, dislike, or discomfort with homosexuals.

It is in this kind of environment that gays and lesbians in
the United States have historically kept their sexuality in the
proverbial "closet." In the 1970s and 1980s, black gay men often
referred to their sexuality with the phrase "in the life," which
became the title of the late Joseph Beam's groundbreaking
anthology of black gay writings. In an era largely defined by
the growing cultural and political influence of the hip-hop generation, the "closet"—a term linked in the minds of many blacks
with *white* homosexuality—has given way to "living on the down
low" or as it is more commonly known "living on the DL." The
term "down low" is a colloquialism that has circulated in black
communities for more than a decade. In its original context,
the phrase was often uttered in reference to sexual infidelity,
perhaps most explicitly represented in the popular R. Kelly
recordings "Down Low (Nobody Has to Know)" (1996) and
"Down Low Double Life" (1998). Many in the black community gained awareness of the down low phenomenon, as applied

to the sexuality of black gay men, via the popular fiction of E. Lynn Harris, beginning with the breakout success of his self-published *Invisible Life* in 1992. Harris, who is openly gay, gave an insider's view (though not necessarily autobiographical) of the DL life for his largely black female audience. As one woman described it, "Sisters were having *Invisible Life* parties, sharing experiences."[17] In many regards, DL has become a metaphoric home-space for black gay men, who cannot build community within traditional gay enclaves or fully express their sexuality in black communities.

In a *New York Times* exposé on the DL phenomenon, Benoit Denizet-Lewis describes black men who embrace the DL identity as "Rejecting a gay culture they perceive as white and effeminate," adding that these men have "settled on a new identity, with its own vocabulary and customs . . . an underground subculture made up of black men who otherwise live straight lives."[18] That the *New York Times* felt compelled to cover black men on the down low was notable in and of itself, because *New York Times* coverage of the AIDS crisis in black communities has been negligent at best though African Americans have accounted for close to forty percent of all HIV cases in the United States. According to the Centers for Disease Control and Prevention (CDC), African Americans also accounted for fifty percent of all the new cases reported in 2002.[19] As Cathy Cohen shows in *Boundaries of Blackness*, despite these high rates of contraction, only five percent of all the stories on AIDS (more than 4500) featured in the *New York Times* between 1983 and 1993 dealt with African Americans. Even more insidiously, a little more than sixty percent of those that did have an African-American angle were focused on the cases of Ervin "Magic" Johnson and Arthur Ashe. I cite this information because the Denizet-Lewis exposé speaks to the extent that "being on the DL" had become another spectacle, evidence of "deviance" for a mainstream public conditioned to think of black people and black men in particular as such. Coverage, like that in the *New*

York Times, in concert with homophobia within the black community, will likely fuel the embrace of DL identities, rather than discourage it.[20]

To suggest that DL identities are simply a response to the homophobia that exists in black communities simplifies the ways in which normative black masculinities are constructed within those communities. Denizet-Lewis suggests that the DL phenomenon is in response to a "black culture that deems masculinity and fatherhood as a black man's primary responsibility—and homosexuality as a white man's perversion."[21] But even Denizet-Lewis's language falls prey to a line of thinking that only conceives of masculinity in terms of a normative heterosexual black identity. Thus some black gay men often publicly express their masculinity within a range of male behaviors deemed acceptable within most black communities. The best example of this is the figure of the homo-thug—black male homosexuals who dress and act in the style of the so-called hip-hop thug in an effort to mask their homosexual identities or to reinforce the image of a black masculinity that challenges the prevailing images of "faggotized" gay men, both black and white. As a regular attendee of The Warehouse, a gay hip-hop club in the Bronx, New York, explained it, "Straight-up homies, niggaz, and thugz can do whatever they want. You can walk through projects and be gay. But you can't walk through the project and be a faggot."[22]

Like E. Lynn Harris, writer James Earl Hardy has made a career sharing the intimacies of black gay culture via novels such as *B-Boy Blues* and *The Day Eazy-E Died*. To represent the impact that hip-hop has had on black gay culture, Hardy describes his protagonists as "homiesexuals." According to Hardy, "These guys I refer to as homie-sexual are, clinically speaking, homosexual. But they very much take on a machismo that separates them from associations with words like *gay*, *queer*, and especially *fag*. I would guess that this has a lot to do with safety, and with a culture that hates you because you're a fag and most definitely because you're black."[23] In an interview in the *Lambda Book Report*, Hardy also challenges the notion that hip-hop culture is itself responsible for the transmission of homophobia within the larger society, asserting that "There have always been homophobic/misogynistic lyrics and statements made by rap acts, but they are not, as some have foolishly argued, integral components of the genre." He adds that the "reason [hip-hop culture] is getting a bad rap is because more white kids are buying rap music, wearing hip-hop fashions, sporting the hairstyles, tripping the language, and publicly lusting after the men and women who are the purveyors of it."[24] Hardy's comments highlight the ways that the demonization of the hip-hop generation intersects with issues of homophobia in the larger society. His work also challenges the perception that hip-hop culture is solely responsible for creating a context in which the homo-thug/DL brother and the black gay and bisexual of the hip-hop generation struggle mightily to find grounding.

The "struggle" is observed in a study published in the *Journal of Sex Research* in which the authors note that African-American gay and bisexual men who possess a "very positive self-identification as being African-American and gay" were likely to experience greater levels of self-esteem and take less sexual risk. In opposition to this were those gay and bisexual black men who were "not able or allowed to simultaneously value their dual identities and be part of both the African-American and gay and lesbian subcultures."[25] In other words, many of the black men of the hip-hop generation who are struggling to integrate their sexual and racial identities are unable to achieve a middle ground. This middle ground is perhaps best expressed in Hardy's assertion that "I don't discuss myself in haves, nor have I measured the level of bigotry thrown at me over the years due to racism or homophobia."[26] Given the extent that black men of the hip-hop generation are marginalized and demonized in American society, it should be no surprise that it would be black gay and bisexual men of the hip-hop generation who would be most adversely affected by the kinds of unsafe sexual practices that foreground the DL crisis.

That young black urban gay males are unable to fuse "ethnic and sexual identity into an integrated whole" speaks to the real impact of homophobia in black communities, including the fear of homophobic retribution, ranging from violent attacks to social isolation.[27] Thus to use the problematic language often used by television personality Judge Greg Mathis, black men who are engaged in sexual acts with men often "man up" in order to mask their sexual identities and be able to remain connected to family and friends. As scholar Rinaldo Walcott states, "When a black man comes out, he has the potential to lose family and friends. White guys can blend into the large white gay community." Walcott adds that "Some blacks who come out have to leave a black environment due to the homophobia which, by the way, is just as [prejudiced] as the dominant society."[28] Artist Glenn Ligon is even more specific arguing that the reason why black men "aren't so cavalier about announcing their sexual orientation is because we need our families. . . . We need our families because of economic reasons, because of racism, because of a million reasons," adding that "if there's the slightest possibility that coming out could disrupt that guys won't do it."[29] Fiction writer Thomas Glave perhaps best captures the politics of black gay men coming out to their families in his short story "The Final Inning." The story centers on the funeral of Duane, a black man on the DL, who is "outed" by a friend during the ceremony. Alluding to the inability of Duane's family to accept the "truth" about his sexuality, Glave writes,[30]

> They all could take the truth about everything else but: about knocked-up teenagers, crack-head sons, numbers-running uncles, raped nieces, drive-by shootings, mixed-race marriages, retarded cousins, rat-filled projects, shitbigoted Koreans, pigfaced skinheads, African famines, Chinese massacres, psycho Jamaicans,

right-wing terrorists, sellout nigger judges, even white-trash serial killers—but not about nobody they cared about supposed to be black and strong like you was Duane but with that faggot shit: what to them was whitefolks shit, another sick nasty fuckedup white thing like that nasty old AIDS, just like nasty whitefolks, not for no black man we know . . .

Glave captures a worldview in which black homosexuality is viewed as more threatening—more dysfunctional—than a host of issues that confront black communities.

Mainstream fascination with the down low was piqued in 2001 when the Centers for Disease Control and Prevention reported that thirty percent of all young black urban men who have sex with men are HIV-positive and that ninety percent of those men are unaware of their infection, as witnessed by the experience of the aforementioned Nushawn Williams. For a generation of young black men who have become accustomed to "death by drive-by," AIDs is now the leading cause of death among African-American men between the ages of twenty-five and forty-four. The CDC specifically cited the DL populace as a factor in the rise of the number of HIV infections among black women who usually contract the disease via *heterosexual* sex acts.[31] The same year the Kaiser Family Foundation esti- mated that sixty-seven percent of black women with AIDS were infected via heterosexual intercourse, up nine percent from 1997.[32] Although the CDC report made clear that there were black men having unprotected sex with other men while main- taining sexual relationships with women, the CDC's linking of the rise of HIV infections among black women to men on the DL creates the perception that there is a clear-cut culprit in the rise of HIV infections in the black community as a whole. David Munar of the AIDs Foundation of Chicago, for example, suggests that the study obscures the continued role of intrave- nous drug use.[33]

The current attempts to demonize gay black men for the rise of HIV infections among black women follows a long-established trend among black media to highlight the impact of the disease on the "weakest" bodies—women and children—within black communities. Cohen highlights the patriarchal aspects associated with the coverage of AIDS by the black press observing that "while black officials were willing to listen to and deploy the personal stories of individual women affected by AIDS, there was a silencing of, and silence among, those who wanted to step out of the model of innocent victim." According to Cohen, "Black women were allowed to speak as long as what they said did not threaten the respectability of community members, in particular black male elites." Of course in much of this early coverage, black gay men were invisible, that is, until the link between black men on the DL and increasing HIV rates among black women was made. The "need to construct black women and black children as community members who need and 'deserve' protection" was now enhanced by an observable scapegoat.[34]

There are indicators that there is a link between rising HIV rates among black women having sex with bisexual black men and black men on the DL, but those "figures" have also proved productive in other ways. I have been struck, for example, by the ways that the DL brother has been used to embolden the image of the black male heterosexual patriarch. For example, as one reporter put it, "Some of those on the 'down low' apparently learned to like sex with men in prison and began dual sex lives after being released, an admission few will ever make, given the power of the black community's taboos against revealing too much and personal concerns about self-preservation." The comment conveniently ignores the issue of male-on-male rape in prison—coyly described as an act of "self-preservation"—but highlights the role of the deviant criminal (the hip-hop thug again) in spreading HIV within the black community. Many of Steve Sternberg's comments were informed by the work of

J.L. King, a self-described recovering DL brother, who earns $10,000 lecture fees for presentations such as "The Five Personality Traits of Down-Low Men" and "Down Low on the Internet." King's motivation seems less about addressing the issue of homophobia which causes some black men into a DL state, but rather to be the "someone in the black community" who says, "Hey man, you're destroying your family." King's message to African-American women is, "If you know your man is having sex with another man, leave him, because he is not going to stop," adding that he feels "so scared for sisters who are now dealing with the invisible black man. We will continue to lose sisters because men will not come out."[35] King's book, *On the Down Low*, was one of the best-selling African-American titles upon its release in mid-2004, but the book did little to stem the tide of homophobia in black communities.

The above comments by King are close to the rhetoric found in black churches, like that of Reverend Calvin Butts, who was once quoted as admonishing his parishioners who lie "about their sexuality, claiming to be heterosexual when they are homosexual or bisexual," adding that they "could be taking home a disease that is fatal to their loved ones."[36] The point here isn't that black men on the DL don't need to be held accountable for infecting unsuspecting black women with the HIV virus— we need to be vigilant on this point—but how the aforementioned comments ignore the fundamental reason why some of these men choose DL identities in the first place. This became clear, again, in early 2004, when the state of North Carolina released a report that identified eighty-four male college students in the state who were recently infected with HIV. Of those eighty-four students, seventy-three were black and among those seventy-three, twenty-seven said they were having sex with male and female partners.[37] Despite efforts to get young black men on the DL to practice safe sex, journalist Cynthia Tucker is right to assert that "No support group or safe-sex counseling would do those young men as much good as broad acceptance of homosexuality." Tucker eloquently adds that "If black America doesn't let go its bigotry, it may end up sacrificing what W.E.B. Du Bois called its talented tenth."[38]

Comments such as those from Butts and King highlight the ways that black men on the DL and others are perceived as selfishly and even purposely spreading disease within the black community, a real perception that men on the DL are trying to undermine the already taxed family structures of the black community. Such thinking was circulated throughout the black community a few years ago when vocalist Peggy Scott-Adams had a hit with the song "Bill." Scott-Adams's song functions much like the literature of James Earl Hardy and E. Lynn Harris, creating sonic space for black women to have a conversation about the DL threat. As Scott-Adams sings in the chorus, "I was ready for Mary, Susan, Helen and Jane, when all the time it was Bill who was sleeping with my man." In the song Scott recalls that Bill was god-uncle to her "only" son, but admits that "now it looks like Uncle Billy wants to be his step-mom." In the context of the song, "Bill" becomes a metaphor for the "destruction" of the black family.

In some cases the DL activities of black men can even be construed as acts driven by forms of misogyny. In a classic example case of "the pot calling the kettle black," this frame of thinking places the onus of misogyny on black gay men, displacing heterosexual black men from the equation. Scholar E. Patrick Johnson makes such an observation in his analysis of "Men On . . .," a popular skit on the ground-breaking black sketch-comedy series *In Living Color*. The "Men On . . ." skits featured two heterosexual actors Damon Wayans and David Allen Grier in the roles of gay critics Blaine and Antoine. The skits often played on the common belief that gay men "hate" women, thus anything that the duo came across that could be seen as women-identified was greeted with a "Hated it." As Johnson argues, "Given the rabid sexism and misogyny espoused by some of the most preeminent black heterosexual leaders of the black community, it is incredible that black heterosexual men would disingenuously project the responsibility of all misogyny onto black gay men, especially in light of black homophobia and its relation to the devaluation of femininity."[39] Although a song like Scott-Adams's or a program like *In Living Color* offers popular insights to how some in the black community may think about the DL phenomenon and homosexuality, it is the Black Church that still remains the dominant voice within black communities, the last line of defense in the minds of many.

One example of this trend is the ministry of Bishop G. E. Patterson, who heads the Church of God in Christ (COGIC). Patterson's sermons have been featured on Black Entertainment Television's (BET) Sunday morning programming over the past few years and it is on the network that I first became aware of him. My wife watched his sermons on a regular basis and I was struck by the number of times I was awakened from my sleep by some of Patterson's homophobic rants; indeed they were as regular as an alarm clock. For all the talk about homophobic rappers, they don't have anything on Patterson. When 40,000 members of COGIC came to Memphis in late 2003 for their annual convocation, Patterson was quoted as saying that "Nobody has the right to be gay." His comments were in response to a decision by the Episcopal church to name an openly gay man as bishop. According to Patterson, "Some would say this is gay bashing, but it's not. . . . I'm not running a popularity contest."[40] He takes a similar stance on the issue of gay marriage, arguing that "Same sex couples are a prelude to the total destruction of our society. . . . No sane person will accept the idea of gay marriage."[41]

The very public debates about gay marriage, including the advocating of constitutional amendments to ban such unions in the United States have provided a forum for black ministers to more widely espouse their concerns about homosexuality. Journalist Ta-Nehisi Coates observes that "Black people vote like Democrats, but on social issues they think like Republicans," and it is with that understanding that right-leaning politicians and activists have sought to exploit what they perceive as a wedge issue between black voters and the Democratic party.[42] This fissure has been most pronounced when framed within discussions of a constitutional amendment to ban gay marriages. For example, black members of the Georgia state legislature found themselves pressured by black clergy in the state to vote in support of an amendment to the state constitution to ban same-sex marriages. According to legislator Al Williams, "Several pastors in my district have contacted me, and I've heard that several other legislators have been called. . . . They want make sure we vote against same-sex marriage."[43] In March of 2004, several of those ministers held a rally in support of the proposed ban. Though gay unions are not recognized in the state of Georgia, the clergy were concerned about the state being forced to recognize unions consummated in other states.

In many of the cases where the black clergy has publicly denounced homosexuality and same-sex marriages, the "truth" of the Bible has been cited as justification for their stance. Reverend Gregory G. Groover, Sr. of the Charles Street AME Church in Boston asserts that "In our political ideology as an oppressed people we will often be against the status quo, but our first call is to hear the voice of God in our scriptures, and where an issue clearly contradicts our understanding of Scripture, we have to apply that understanding."[44] According to Triette Reeves, who is a minister at Detroit's Mount Zion Church of God, as well as a member of the Michigan House of Representatives, "From the African-American perspective, which is the only perspective I can give, our focus is, 'God said it, we believe it, and we should promote it.' I know it sounds elementary but it's really that simple." In response to Reeves's assertion, *Washington Post* columnist Jabari Asim, quipped, "Reeves's comments left me with two questions: Where were you when God 'said' this to you? What do you mean 'we'?"[45] Cynthia Tucker adds, "It is disappointing to see black ministers—several of whom are old enough to remember the lash of Jim Crow—brandishing the Bible against gays the same way Bull Connor wielded a billy club against civil rights marchers."

Black theologian Kelly Brown Douglas notes that there is a specific context for the position that many black clergy take with regard to homosexuality and the "word of God." Douglas writes that "With such a history of the Bible being used against us, it seems abhorrent that some Blacks would steadfastly use the Bible against others," but notes that "It is a reflection of the judicious sense of biblical authority that was born during the period of enslavement and honed throughout the history of the Black struggle in the United States."[46] "Even though they were not permitted to learn to read or write or encounter the Bible independently from their enslavers," Douglas observes, "Africans found ways to experience the power of the Bible for themselves, primarily through an oral tradition." She adds, "A distinct understanding of biblical authority emerged as part of this oral tradition, and it determined two things; which stories were passed down, and how they were interpreted. . . . Those that survived were the passages that were most compatible with Black life, that spoke to Black people's deepest aspirations for freedom, dignity, justice, and vindication."[47] Douglas admits that "Our homophobic views have driven our reading of the Bible, rather than the Bible shaping our views," but asserts that "In order to mitigate biblically-based Black homophobia, a meaningful discussion of the Bible and sexuality, specifically homosexuality, will have to emerge from the black community itself. Such a discussion must take place within the wider context [of] Black people's own struggle for life and wholeness."[48] Douglas's prescription is best represented in the query, "Does the text support the life and freedom of all Black people?"[49] Such an empowering logic helps to counter ridiculous claims like that of Chicago minister Reverend Gregory Daniels, who at a press conference asserted that "If the K.K.K. opposes gay marriage, I would ride with them."[50]

Still others fall back on the classic retort that same-sex marriage helps further the "destruction" of black families. For example, Bishop Gilbert A. Thompson Sr., head of the largest Protestant congregation in Massachusetts, suggests that black ministers are "weighing in on [gay marriage] because we're concerned with the epidemic rate of fatherlessness in America and in our community, and we don't [think] gay marriage helps that cause."[51] Thompson's comments of course discount the possibility that black gay men can be and *are* fathers and in effect insinuate that the debate over gay marriage is really an issue for white gay communities. Hip-hop theologian Reverend Osagyefo Uhuru Sekou points to the irony of such thinking, asking pointedly, "Why would a brother in a monogamous relationship with another gay brother be shunned while the promiscuous preacher is celebrated Sunday after Sunday?"[52] In another example, longtime civil rights activist and former Washington, D.C. representative Walter Fauntroy says he's "unalterably opposed to anything other than an institution for two purposes, the socialization of children and the perpetuation of the species."[53] Fauntroy is a prominent member of the Alliance for Marriage, which has tactically recruited the black clergy in their efforts to gain support for a constitutional amendment banning same-sex marriages.[54]

Fauntroy's concerns about black homosexuality became public record over twenty years ago. As National Director of the 1983 March on Washington, essentially a twentieth-anniversary celebration of the 1963 march, Fauntroy was approached by the leadership of the National Coalition of Black Gays (NCBG), requesting the inclusion of a lesbian or gay platform speaker at the march. On behalf of the New Coalition of Conscience, a group of traditional civil rights organizations, peace advocates, labor unions, clergy, and feminist groups who sponsored the march, Fauntroy, according to Alexis DeVeaux, expressed concern that the "issue of gay rights was a divisive one within the [coalition]. He also worried publicly that an official endorsement of gay rights might be viewed as advocating homosexuality."[55]

After some pressure from NCBG, Fauntroy and the New Coalition of Conscience allowed noted poet Audre Lorde to address the gathering, even though they initially requested that she read remarks scripted by the organizers, a request that Lorde rejected. According to DeVeaux, after her three-minute address, Lorde told a reporter that "She felt her three minutes were a defining moment for the black civil rights movement, the lesbian and gay movement, and for the recognition of lesbians and gay men of color."[56] As a self-defined "black, lesbian, feminist, mother, poet warrior," Lorde explicitly understood the way that race, gender, and sexuality intersected in the lives of black men and women. This intersectionality is unfortunately lost on some of the black clergy who are against same-sex marriages as witnessed by the comments of Reverend Eugene Rivers, who argues that "There's always been this undercurrent, from the women's movement through other movements, that the history of black people and their struggle was being opportunistically appropriated by an assortment of groups when it was convenient," adding that the gay marriage movement is "particularly offensive because it hits at the Book, at the Bible, and the painful history of black people all at once."[57] In the context of River's logic, the struggle of black gays and lesbians, who still are "pained" by the homophobia that circulates within black communities is discounted.

Baby Girl Drama, Baby Girl Tragedy: Remembering Sakia Gunn

The willingness of black clergy and black national leadership to speak out against same-sex marriage and the threats that DL brothers pose to the black community has to be juxtaposed to the relative silence among those same men in response to homophobic violence. One of the best examples was the national response to the murder of fifteen-year-old Sakia Gunn. Gunn was returning home from a night on the town in New York City with a few of her female friends. As they waited under a bus shelter in their hometown of Newark, New Jersey at 3:30 A.M. they were approached by two men in a car, who apparently saw the young women as sexual prey. In an attempt to discourage their advances, Gunn informed the pair that she and her friends were lesbians and thus not interested. A scuffle ensued and Richard McCullough, age 29, reportedly stabbed Gunn in the heart. Gunn died at a local hospital shortly thereafter. Though Gunn's murder received some coverage in the *Newark Star-Ledger*, the *New York Times*, gay organs such as *The Advocate* and *Gay City News*, and on CNN, there was little commentary about her death in the black community. That silence spoke both to the homophobia that is part of the very fabric of black life in America—aiding and abetting the decision of the black mainstream press to ignore or give little attention to Gunn's murder—and the black community's continued willingness to close ranks around black men, particularly when they prey on women and children.

Writing for the online journal *The Gully*, Kelly Cogswell and Ana Simo admit that there were "fundamental errors in the way most journalists reported the brutal May 11 murder of Sakia Gunn." For example they cite the seeming collusion among reporters to highlight the "scuffle" that occurred between Gunn and her murderer, with the implication being that if Gunn and her friends had not openly antagonized the men by announcing their sexual orientation, the men would have left them alone. According to Cogswell and Simo, "It's far more likely that the men only propositioned Gunn and her friends because they knew the girls were dykes, and a sexual advance would provoke some kind of exchange."[58] Longtime activists Alicia Banks is even more to the point suggesting that because Gunn "appeared to be masculine, she probably evoked even more hatred in insecure 'men.' . . . Such gaybashing excuses for real men, fear butch lesbians who dare to embrace the masculinity that eludes their own fragile egos and weak sexual identities."[59]

Ironically, McCullough was raised by his maternal grandmother, who was reportedly a lesbian.

Although it is perhaps easy to suggest that Gunn's murder was an isolated example of gay bashing, such an interpretation obscures the relationship between sexuality and gender. Gay men are often "bashed" because of an affinity to women and lesbians are bashed because they *are* women. In many regards homophobia is rooted in misogyny, a hatred of women. Too often forms of sanitized and user-friendly sexism and misogyny circulate throughout black communities in the silence around black male violence against black women and girls. Although Cogswell and Simo suggest that homophobia is the reason that Newark's black mayor Sharpe James initially gave only lip service to Gunn's family and supporters in the aftermath of her murder or for his unwillingness to intervene on behalf of students of West Side High School in Newark (where Gunn was a student) who were denied the opportunity by the school's principal to organize a memorial on her behalf, it is not always that simple. Had McCullough been a white man (or a police officer), is there any doubt that Gunn's death would have been a national controversy?

As legal scholar Devon Carbado describes this reality, black men are "up in arms when white men abuse Black women because they want it known that Black women's bodies will no longer be the terrain for white male physical or sexual aggression," but adds that "When the abuser is a Black male, the response is less politically strident . . . because the assault is on the Black woman. Even if ultimately criticized and condemned, it is sometimes understood to represent an assertion of Black male masculinity, which, is argued, is a response to white male racism."[60] This explains, in part, why some in the black community have sought to vigorously rehabilitate the images of well-known black men like Mike Tyson, R. Kelly, and even the late Tupac Shakur when they were accused of sexually abusing black women and girls. It also explains, in part, why stories such as that of Sakia Gunn or Cherae Williams, who in September of 1999 was brutally beaten by two New York City police officers after she accused them of failing to intervene in a domestic dispute with her black boyfriend, get pushed to the back pages of our newspapers and journals.[61] Of course it's not as if young black men and boys aren't sexually abused by black women and men; we need only look at the tragic circumstances of the young Antwone Fisher. But where Fisher was allowed to tell his story, first in a best-selling book and later on the big-screen, there is the example of filmmaker Aishah Shahidah Simmons, who a decade after she began work on her documentary *NO!*, which examines black male sexual violence against women, was still trying to raise funds to complete her film.

Of course the white media is not totally blameless in this silence either. Cogswell and Simo bemoan the "tendency to blame only white racism for the general invisibility of Sakia Gunn's murder" but the reality is that Gunn's death has disappeared because the white mainstream press is *at best* indifferent to the death of black people at the hands of other black people.[62] At worst the white mainstream press is driven by the racist reality that black life (and death) has little value to them as journalists and pundits. It is not a relevant news story. For example, when Elizabeth Smart was abducted from her home in June of 2002, her disappearance became a national obsession.[63] Most Americans were unaware that a seven-year-old black girl, Alexis Patterson, had been missing for a month.[64] It would be two weeks still after the abduction of Smart and seemingly minute-by-minute updates by the national news media, that the national media (CNN) would finally interview Patterson's mother.[65] More than two years later, Patterson is still missing, leading journalist Eugene Kane to write, "If Hussein can be found, surely so can Alexis?" referencing the Iraqi leader who was found hiding in a hole by U.S. troops.

Kim Pearson, a professor of journalism at the College of New Jersey, has in fact done research comparing the coverage of Gunn's death to that of Matthew Shepard, who was murdered in a gay-bias attack in 1998. Using the Lexis–Nexis database, Pearson has uncovered that there were 692 stories in major newspapers regarding Shepard's murder, compared to only 22 stories—22—about Gunn's murder in the seven-month period after their attacks. Pearson also notes that not only were Shepard's attackers tried and convicted during that period, but that it took nearly that long for Gunn's accused murderer to even be indicted.[66] Black folk have of course for a long time understood the indifference of the white mainstream press to our issues, hence the historical importance of the independent black press (and in some cases the independent white press) and this is why it is so disheartening that too many of them had failed (including this writer) to give Gunn's murder and the implications that it has for our communities the attention it deserves.

As I've suggested previously, I make no claims that I am the product of any enlightened sense of the sexual dramas that confront our communities. I am in continuous struggle with my own homophobia and sexism, but it has been my two daughters, aged five years and eighteen months, that have helped me see why it's important to speak out against attacks such as the one on Sakia Gunn and to speak *back* to the silence surrounding such attacks. I have no idea what kinds of sexualities my daughters will ultimately embrace, but it is my hope that they will be able to express their identities, sexual or otherwise, without fear of violent repercussions, physical or rhetorical. I hope that they too will be comfortable with taking anti-homophobic stances in their civic and professional lives. I'd like to think that as young girls and women they will be able to flow freely through society without being the prey of men, black or otherwise, who have little respect for women. And in all honesty it is largely because of the challenges faced with raising young black girls in a racist, sexist, misogynistic, and homophobic society that I even began to really embrace the politics that I so hope to instill in my daughters.

Chapter 4

bringing up daddy

---

a black feminist fatherhood

She gonna be somebody/Instead of somebody's baby-mama

De La Soul, "Trying People"

My wife Gloria and I were heartbroken. I was at a conference
in Houston when she finally got through to me by cell phone to
tell me the news that all potential adoptive parents dread. Folk
privy to the adoption process are all too familiar with the possibility that at the last hour, a woman, who months earlier agreed
to give her unborn child up for adoption, will take one look at
her newborn baby and change her mind. My wife and I kept
our impending adoption a secret from just about everyone
including parents, close friends, and even our then-four-year-
old daughter, for that very reason. So here I was alone, on the
brink of tears, walking through an FAO Schwarz toy store in
Houston, looking at the toys and stuffed animals I wasn't going

to buy for our newborn daughter. I was also relieved. Camille Monet, as we had planned to name the newborn girl, was to be our second adopted child. My wife and I had talked for some time about adopting a second child, but the reality was that I wasn't looking forward to having another baby in the house. The often-prohibitive cost of adoption conspired to keep Misha Gabrielle our only child, as I looked forward to giving her all of the love and support that comes with being an only child (as I was). My ambivalence about adopting a second child caused me to revisit my hesitancy to adopt four years earlier.

My wife and I were among the millions of couples whose difficulties with conception meant hours of testing, manufactured copulation, and the prospect of costly in vitro fertilization, none of which guaranteed that we would become pregnant. Though I had resisted (ignored really) my wife's suggestion that we consider adoption, I finally relented and agreed to take a "look see" at the process. Adoption was always a last resort and one that I was prepared to be just that, as we waited for the research around in vitro fertilization to improve to the point that it was more of a viable option for us. In our early thirties then, my wife was unwilling to wait and in one tear-filled episode finally convinced me that adoption was our only option. At the time I guess I was like so many black men, who viewed the process of getting a women pregnant as an affirmation of our masculinity—think of how many black men describe their kids as their seeds—particularly in a society that has historically denied us the fullest expression of our masculinity. Thus the idea that I couldn't produce "seed" somehow meant that something was wrong with me, that I was less than a man. As Thaddeus Goodavage rhetorically asks about the impact of adoption on black men, "How does a Black man, already disaffirmed and demasculated by the wider society, affirm his own manhood when he cannot create, produce, or sustain anything, even children?"[1] As long as we didn't adopt, I could always say that our childlessness was a "lifestyle choice."

My visions of fatherhood, and manhood for that matter, were naturally influenced by the black man I called "Daddy." Old-school in every sense of the word, from his Georgia-bred slowness and assortment of Old Spice bottles, to the way he counted his money (in the dark while my mother and I slept), I can't say that my father taught me anything about fatherhood other than the fact that a good father—a good man—put in a day's work and provided for his family. Legal scholar Nancy E. Dowd observes that "The most critical way of proving one's masculinity is by being an economic provider, and it is precisely in that respect that Black men are denied the means to be men in traditional terms."[2] And that was indeed a mantra for my father, who most of my childhood trekked three hours, back and forth to work every day from the Bronx to Brooklyn, where he worked twelve-hour days, six days a week as a short-order cook and dishwasher at a combination drugstore and grill in Crown Heights. On most days, Daddy was out the house before I woke and didn't get home until I was fast asleep. Save Friday and Saturday nights in the summer when he allowed me to walk with him to the bodega to get beer, cigarettes, pork rinds, and the Hostess cupcakes I craved and the Sunday mornings when he shared the sounds of the Mighty Clouds of Joy, The Dixie Hummingbirds, B.B. King, and Bobby "Blue" Bland with me and allowed me to help him with Sunday morning breakfast, I can't say that I remember my father as a parenting presence. Certainly he was of a generation of men who accepted that things like changing diapers, boiling bottles, and making formula was considered *women's* work. And my mother held out no other expectations of him, save the occasional request to mop the kitchen floor or wash the dishes.

Because adoption caused me to reassess my ideas of what black manhood meant—as if our only value in the world was to get women pregnant, make money, and provide patriarchal leadership in our families and communities—I was also forced to reconsider what roles fathers play in the parenting process.

Sociologist Sandra Walker acknowledges, "When children see their father wash dishes, clothes, and become involved in school activities, it presents a broader and more positive picture of what a black man can be."[3] Though I had considered myself a feminist long before I became a father, it was the birth and adoption of my daughter that forced me to understand that a shared parenting process was as important as notions that women should get equal pay for equal work. We give children very little credit for being able to discern that the division of labor between "mommy" and "daddy" in the household is often reflective of the value accorded "mommy" and "daddy" in the real world. Thus a woman's work is that of the professional nurturer, whether at home, at childcare facilities, primary schooling, or in the workforce.

Examining the impact that childcare activities can have on men, sociologist Scott Coltrane argues that "Given women's biological capacity to bear and nurse children, men's participation in early childcare necessarily entails a minimum level of male-female cooperation. Sharing child-rearing tasks probably creates expectations for male-female cooperation in other, more public, activities and may enhance women's opportunities to exercise public authority."[4] Not only does the sharing of childcare activities help provide a more egalitarian view of how gender functions in the "real" world, it also has the potential to help young children embrace those views. My daughter, for example, has never expressed the idea that there are things that "Daddy does" or "Mommy does," because she sees us sharing or rotating everyday childcare activities, though that hasn't kept her from expressing a preference for my wife's cooking ("Daddy, you always make chicken!").

It certainly wasn't easy. I've never been dutiful about picking up after myself and my wife has always had to prod me (sometimes under threats of violence) to do things like mop the kitchen floor or even take out the trash. And I guess that somewhere in my upbringing I accepted that housework, including childcare, was the kind of domestic work that was naturally assigned to the women in the house. Virtually every family-oriented television show I've watched over the last thirty-eight years, from *I Love Lucy* to *Roseanne* confirms the perception that women were naturally endowed domestics, giving some support to my mother's quips during my childhood that she was more than a "glorified maid." Sociologists Coltrane and Masako Ishii-Kuntz suggest that there are specific contexts when men begin to wrap their heads around the concept of shared domestic work, notably when husbands and wives delay having children and "in response to the husband's ideology and time availability." According to the researchers, "husbands' less traditional gender/family ideology and fewer employment hours were strong predictors of their performing more mundane and routine family work."[5] In the context of my own life my views as a feminist and my career as a writer and academic provided the circumstances in which I was at least open to the idea of sharing "mundane" housework when my wife and I first decided to adopt.

In steps the brown-skinned shortie, who we affectionately referred to as the "baby-girl diva" after spending a few short months with her. No one ever believes our story, but less than one month (twenty-five days officially) from the time we walked into the adoption agency, got a few brochures, and took home an application, we were bringing seventeen-day-old Misha Gabrielle into our home. The quickness of the adoption process is in part due to that tragic state of black adoption: potential white parents often wait as long as three years (hence the sudden focus on interracial adoption, particularly of Asian newborns), while newborn black babies often languish for months in foster care until adoptive parents are found. Needless to say, we were (especially me) absolutely unprepared for parenthood. To be honest, I had come to enjoy the freedom that our childless existence allowed, and as an up-and-coming black scholar, I relished the time that I could spend in Starbucks getting my "read and write" on. My wife sensed very early after we were

made aware of Misha's birth and the possibility that we could
adopt her, that I was hesitant and issued to me an ultimatum that
shall remain unrepeated (my wife has a gift for witty venom).

Misha Gabrielle was born a preemie, coming into the world
three weeks before she was supposed to be here. I was in the
car one day listening to N'dea Davenport's "Placement for the
Baby" (a song about adoption whose lyrics I really hadn't listened closely to) and I literally broke down thinking about
what kind of spirit this baby-girl possessed that she willed
herself into the world three weeks early. It's like she *knew* we
were the adoptive parents she was supposed to be with and
forced herself into the world before schedule, just so *we* would
be the ones to adopt her. It would be the first glimpse that I
would have of the baby-girl diva's independent spirit and the
first of many life lessons that she would teach me during her
now six year-old life. In the classic narratives associated with
adoption, it is always about what the adoptive parents bring to
the table, as they are often seen as "rescuing" a child, particularly black children, from a life of poverty and neglect. But with
Misha Gabrielle it has always been about what *she* brings to the
table. I can honestly say that she has fundamentally changed my
life. The very spirit that brought her into the world early, she
brought to her role as my daughter as if it was her ordained duty
to make me an engaged father *and* a better man.

But Misha's impact on me was so much deeper. Yes she would
make me a better man, but she also saved my life. For more
than a decade I had suffered with what could only be described
as an earth-shattering snore. Soon that snoring was accompanied by sudden waking episodes during my nighttime sleep and
morning headaches. It wasn't until I began inexplicably falling
asleep during the course of the day that I gave any thought that
perhaps something was awry. By the time Misha was in the mix
I was deep in the throes of a ginseng addiction, somehow believ-
ing that my sleeping *and* waking problems were the product of
my undernourishing my over-250-pound frame. Unbeknownst

to me at the time, these were all the classic signs of sleep apnea (apnea is Greek for "without breath"), a condition in which folks awake suddenly from their sleep several times a night after they have *stopped* breathing for small periods of time, often as long as a minute. The disease causes a restless sleep, which the body attempts to compensate for during the course of the day while those who suffer from the disease sit quietly behind a desk, watch TV on the couch, and most tragically are behind the wheels of moving vehicles. According to the American Sleep Apnea Association an estimated ten million Americans have unrecognized sleep apnea.[6] What this all meant for me was that when my sleep apnea was combined with the general sleeplessness that comes with having a newborn in the house, I was for all intents a walking zombie.

I have vivid memories of two early morning feedings with my daughter, then still very much an infant, where I fell asleep only to awaken a half-hour later with her fast asleep on the floor where I had apparently dropped her. (I just got around to sharing that story with my wife about a year ago.) At four- or five-months old my rather precocious daughter was apparently already hip to the deal and would often smack me across the face when I fell asleep while we played on the couch. The stories of Mark falling asleep during mid-conversation or snoring loud enough to be heard across the street were humorous at the time, but were no longer funny when my still-undiagnosed sleep apnea often caused me to doze off while behind the wheel of the car. As my daughter's childcare was five minutes from the campus where I taught at the time, it meant that most often she was in the car with me as I struggled to stay awake. It was after a small fender-bender that I finally got serious about the sleep problem and went the local sleep center to be tested. Shortly thereafter, I was hooked up to an array of apparatuses and my sleep was monitored overnight. The morning after my sleep patterns were monitored, the attending technician informed me that I had seven hundred apneic events. I stopped breathing seven hundred times during the course of a six-hour "sleep." In other words I had a "severe" case of sleep apnea, one that if left untreated would likely end up with me having a heart attack or stroke while still in my early thirties. Sleep apnea is caused when air passages are closed shut during sleep, causing those afflicted with the condition to gasp for air during their sleep, hence the loud snoring sounds and sudden waking. Sleep apnea is generally caused by obesity. Men, people with large necks, and young African Americans are part of the likely at-risk group. Besides daytime drowsiness, there is a noticeable dropoff in motor skills, short-term memory, and the development of a less-than-engaging personal disposition.

Together for more than ten years, my wife often commented, at the time, that I had changed. It is a comment, along with complaints of snoring, often made by the partners of those who suffer from severe cases of sleep apnea. A few months after my sleep test I began receiving treatment for my sleep apnea. Treatment meant wearing a mask to bed, even during quick naps. The mask is connected to a machine known as a CPAP (continuous positive airway pressure), which pushes air into my nose keeping my air passages open and allowing me to have a restful sleep. The machine is small enough to fit in a shoulder bag, thus easy to travel with. When on business trips, very often the first thing I do when I get to a hotel is to identify an outlet close to the bed to plug in my CPAP. The morning after I was first hooked up the CPAP I remember telling my wife that it was like I had been born again. My doctor at the sleep center cautioned that a significant number of folks don't recover sufficiently because they do not consistently use the machine because of discomfort and other factors including forgetfulness. I can honestly say that after that first night of sleep, I can't imagine ever being without my CPAP. In the months after I began treatment it was like Misha and I were both newborns trying to make sense of the world. In my mind, I should have died while Misha was still a baby, but my life was saved by a little brown girl who willed herself into the world and then willed herself into her daddy's heart. What did my wife and I bring to the table? Yeah, we brought a stable home and a loving environment, but it was my daughter who brought me life.

It was in the context of all of these events that I really began to take the idea of fatherhood, even in a traditional sense, very seriously. The demands of my wife's own professional career often meant that I couldn't simply see myself as a part-time baby-sitter (as one brother once described spending time with his kids) or the one who just picked up our daughter from school—the kinds of things that most fathers do regularly at one time or another—but as a co-nurturer. I remember the very first day my wife left me alone with Misha. Gloria had returned to work after taking a month-long maternity leave and we decided that the days that I didn't teach, I would stay home with Misha instead of sending her to daycare. I remember meticulously picking out the music that I wanted her to listen to as we sat at home that day, beginning with Marvin Gaye and Tammi Terrell's "Ain't No Mountain High Enough" and "You're All I Need to Get By" which I quietly sung in her tiny ear. Truth be told, once the romance died off, it was something that I could not sustain (the sleep apnea was kicking my ass) and months later Misha was in daycare full-time. Nevertheless, for most of my daughter's life I have prepared the family dinner, done the grocery shopping, given her nightly baths, and put her down to sleep at night, things I can rarely remember my own father doing. Granted my dad's work schedule made such things impossible, but as I noted, there was never an expectation that he would be a more engaged parent. Both my parents were the products of a generation of people who really believed that black men were incapable of playing such a role, so even when those women felt imposed upon at times, there was little drama. I'm not saying that all black families functioned this way thirty years ago, but it was clearly an accepted trend.

The fact that so many black fathers weren't expected to be involved fathers speaks to an underlying "father bias" that exists in the larger society and often discourages men from playing such roles. In their book *Throwaway Dads*, child psychologists Ross D. Parke and Armin A. Brott observe that stereotypes that "Dads are lazy, dangerous, biologically unfit or deadbeats powerfully shapes our impressions about fathers."[7] The authors also note that within children's literature, "Fathers, if they're shown at all, are generally portrayed as indifferent, uncaring, buffoonish characters who do little more than come home late after work and bounce baby around for five minutes before putting her to bed."[8] For example, the very reason we all found a film like Eddie Murphy's *Daddy Daycare* so damn funny was because the idea that a group of men would run a childcare facility is utterly preposterous to our sensibilities. Yes, the men in the film were challenged to run a daycare facility, as any novice childcare worker would be regardless of gender, but the subtext of the film was that we found these men incapable of being engaged fathers. Because of my flexible work hours as a college professor and writer, I was often the one charged with daycare duty and sick days and it was during those many, many hours riding around in my old Honda Accord listening to *Veggie Tales* tapes, and the music of Lenny Kravitz, or sitting in Starbucks reading Faith Ringgold picture books (*Tar Beach* in particular) or any of the books in David Kirk's *Miss Spider* series (Miss Spider was adopted), or playing tackle in the living room that we formed the ultimate father–daughter bond. I began to refer to her as my "Soul Sister." But it was also in this context that I began to deal first-hand with issues of "father bias."

I've found myself offended, for example, on those occasions that folk assume that the time I put in with and for my daughter is somehow an aberration. There are those times when I go into children's clothing stores (*Children's Place* is a favorite of mine) to buy a cute pair of shoes or a sweater for my daughter and the salesperson will doggedly ask me if I need help (the assumption being that I couldn't possibly know anything about children's sizes, let alone the clothing size of my own child and no doubt complicated by the fact that I'm black), or if I want a gift-box as if the only reason why a man would be in a store like that was because he was buying a gift. Then there are the daycare providers who never feel the need the share the intricacies of my daughter's day, but offer them gratuitously to my wife whenever she does pick-up. In his book *The Nurturing Father*, Kyle D. Pruett observes the ways fathers are sometimes treated when they accompany their children to doctor's appointments. As one pediatrician told Pruett, "I just thought the father was doing the 'well-baby visit' as an interested escort."[9] And then there are the subtleties, like the general lack of baby-changing stations in men's public restrooms or the great drama of being the only man—and more often than not the only black—in a room full of mothers at my daughter's various extracurricular activities. Political scientist and feminist dad Isaac Balbus recalls his feelings while accompanying his daughter once to her weekly playgroup: "I feared that a male would not be entirely welcome at an otherwise entirely female affair. This was 'women's space' into which I was not inclined to intrude. . . . I was received cordially, but it seemed to me that there was little, if anything, to talk about."[10] And like Balbus, I am cordially received, but there is also a discomfort, likely informed by the fact that most of the white women who are in the room have rarely had a conversation with a black man who wasn't serving them in some capacity.

Even worse are those folk want to bestow the Nobel Peace Prize of parenting on me simply because they've never seen a black man as a "good" parent. When the wife of one of my colleagues once remarked to me that she had never seen a man so attentive to his child, I wasn't quite sure whether she was talking about men in general or black men in particular, especially because I saw her husband as a man who was particularly attentive to his son. Throughout their book Parke and Brott often compare the stereotypical treatment that fathers face in American society to that of African Americans, arguing that "It's humiliating, degrading, and ultimately psychologically damaging."[11] Although I would challenge the full weight of such a comparison, what does their analysis say about the ways that society views *black* fathers? And I have to admit there are times that I have to resist patting myself on the back for doing the kinds of things that society would have us believe black men were genetically challenged to do. What I do is not exceptional; it comes with the territory of being a parent in the twenty-first century. When I talk with so many of my friends and colleagues who are fathers—half of my conversations with fellow "hip-hop scholar" S. Craig Watkins are about our daughters—or see the number of public figures who alter their lifestyles so that their children can be part of their professional lives, I realize that there are many black men who are dramatically altering the larger society's views of black men as parents.

One good example of this trend is baseball manager Dusty Baker and his relationship with his young son Darren. When managing the San Francisco Giants a few years ago, Baker allowed the children of his players (most often boys) to have a visible presence in the clubhouse and in the dugout. The sons of a few of his players at the time, including Barry Bonds's son, Nikolai, and Darren Baker, rotated as team batboys. In the eyes of many, the normally surly Bonds became human—even endearing—as he kissed his son Nikolai at home plate after hitting home runs. But it was Darren Baker, who was only three years old when he served as the Giants' batboy in the last two months of 2002, who was the most endearing. But Dusty Baker's parenting skills were called into question during the 2002 World Series, when Darren Baker ran out on the field during a game. The young boy was saved from being in the middle of a possible collision at home plate, when the Giants' J.T. Snow grabbed him by the back of his collar and pulled him out of danger.

At the time of the incident Baker was fifty-three-years old and less than a year removed from a bout with prostate cancer. Given his career he understood he wasn't always going to be around to be a regular presence in his young son's life, so he instead chose to have his son come to "work" with him, particularly in the years before Darren was school age.[12] The first thing Baker did, after the Giants lost the final game of the 2002 World Series was to reach down and console his crying son. It's the kind of image we rarely see of black fathers in American society.

Unknown to many folks though, Baker's decision to have Darren around may have also been in response to his own estranged relationship with his father earlier in his baseball career. Johnny Baker, Sr. had been an influence on Dusty Baker as a youth, often coaching him in Little League, but the two fell out when the younger Baker was drafted by the Atlanta Braves in 1967 and signed a contract with the team against his father's wishes. When his father attempted to challenge the signing in court, Dusty Baker cut his ties with him. As a seventeen-year old playing professional sports and being away from his family for the first time, Baker sought out another father figure, finding him in the figure of Henry Aaron. When Aaron went through a divorce and lamented about missing his children, Baker re-evaluated his relationship with his father. According to sportswriter Tom Stanton, "For years, Baker had little or nothing to do with his father. He didn't call him, and he didn't include him in his life. . . . But seeing how much Aaron missed his children helped open his eyes, and it was one of the factors among several that led him to reconnect with his own father."[13] The weekend after the San Francisco Giants lost the 2002 World Series, Dusty Baker accompanied his then seventy-seven-year-old father to a Notre Dame football game, telling reporters, "It's something he always wanted to do."[14]

Dusty Baker's relationship with his father and son highlight the significance we have placed in American society, and black communities specifically, on the relationship between fathers and their sons and on fatherhood and masculinity. As Goodavage asserts, "Fathering a biological son provides a certain space to celebrate intergenerationally and genetically. In the elite context of biological father-son relationships, maleness—that sacrosanct quality grounded on falsely constructed notions of power— moves along uncriticized, as father essentially remakes himself in another who closely resembles him."[15] Journalist Jonetta Rose Barras, who examines fatherlessness in the lives of black women in her book *Whatever Happened to Daddy's Little Girl?* adds that "Most of the data on fatherlessness in America captures the effect on boys and men, little of it references girls and women."[16] I have no qualms with "celebrating" the impact that engaged black fathers have on their sons, but in the spirit of the issues that I've consistently raised in this book, the "patri- archal" focus of those relationships often obscures the impact that black fathers can and do have on their daughters. In this case I'm not just talking about little black girls seeing their fathers as strong, protective, and responsive to their needs and the needs of their family and community—absolutely laudable attributes for any daughter to have access to—but a black father- hood that attempts to embody, to the extent that a man can, the realities of being a young black girl and woman in American society. In other words I am calling for a black feminist father- hood that not only has an impact upon the lives of black girls and women, but is also tied to a reconsideration of what black masculinity can be.

In her book *Redefining Fatherhood*, Dowd argues that "Men's identities as fathers do not exist in isolation from their identi- ties as men. Indeed, that broader masculine identity arguably poses the most difficult challenge to a redefined and differently lived fatherhood. As long as masculinity identifies nurture and care as feminine and unmanly, men's socialization will work against them rather than for them."[17] Other scholars and psy- chologists also support the notion that fathers must embrace the idea of being a nurturer. According to Pruett, "The only way for many men to find nurturing quality in themselves is to stop restricting and strangling it—to allow it to come forward," adding that "A father may embrace his children, but until he embraces his own unique, irreplaceable value to them as a parent, he does not have as much in his arms as he thinks."[18] Psychologist Louise Silverstein takes it a step further arguing that the "experience of nurturing and caring for young children has the power to change the cultural construction of masculinity, into something less coercive and oppressive for both women and men."[19]

Many black women have discussed the importance of their relationships with their fathers, particularly in the context of their father's absences, because of work or other more dramatic issues. Qubilah Shabazz, who witnessed the assassination of her father Malcolm X (El-Hajj Malik El-Shabazz) in 1965, sweetly recalls her father's presence: "He almost had me convinced that I was made up of brown sugar. . . . Every morning, he'd take my finger and stir his coffee with my finger. He said it was to sweeten it up."[20] In her book *When Chickenheads Come Home to Roost: My Life as a Hip-Hop Feminist*, journalist and critic Joan Morgan writes, "From the ages of four to seven I cried inconsolably each time my father left the house. No one knew quite what to make of this. I was too young to understand the dangers that lurked outside our South Bronx apartment, and because my father didn't keep odd, inexplicable hours, my tantrums were dismissed as the unbridled passion of first love."[21] Reflecting on her own childhood of fatherlessness, Jonetta Rose Barras wrote that a "girl abandoned by the first man in her life forever entertains powerful feelings of being unworthy or incapable of receiving any man's love. Even when she receives love from another, she is constantly and intensely fearful of losing it. This is the anxiety, the pain, of losing one father. I had three fathers toss me aside."[22]

In many ways, Rose Barras's admission helps highlight the common thinking that young black girls and women are in need of strong patriarchal figures in their life, but there are other examples of black women who discuss the absence of black fathers in their lives in ways that speak more broadly to the impact of nurturance. For example, even though the parents of literary scholar and activist Sharon Patricia Holland divorced when she was seven years old and her father, who was a doctor, wasn't always a presence in her life, she recalls a time when "This woman came in because her daughter was bleeding uncontrollably. My Dad treated her, called the ambulance and when the woman tried to pay him, he put his hand around hers and held her. I'll never forget that moment—although I knew he wasn't always there for me—I also knew that he was caring about black women often left behind by their families, communities and the District of Columbia. I carry that image of him with me and conjure it often—especially in those moments when I want to walk away, or when I want to be angry at him for something."[23] Morgan recalls a father who was "a serious womanizer" and "pretty chauvinistic in some senses when it came to mom, he totally didn't support her dreams and visions of higher education, travel . . . and expected total support for his. And I can honestly say he is the source of all of my abandonment and commitment issues of which I have many." But she admits, "On the other hand, he adored me and there is something to be said for being a daddy's girl. . . . And he really believed, or at least made me believe I could be Prime Minister of Jamaica one day if I wanted and I think he would have really been thrilled if I'd gone to law school and went into politics. I NEVER got the message that I couldn't do anything because I was a girl."[24]

Parke and Brott argue that girls have "a lot to gain emotionally, socially, intellectually, and psychologically from greater contact with their fathers."[25] This point is reinforced by Nicole Johnson who says, "I can't imagine who I would be without my father . . . my father was my primary caretaker from about 2–4 [years of age] because he worked nights. . . . I consider my father one of my best friends," adding that "He has always been accessible to me. . . . He always told me the truth even when I didn't want to hear it [and] he had faith in the way he raised me to go out in the world and not mess up too much."[26] Literary scholar Daphne Brooks is even more specific about the role her father, a public school administrator and activist, had on her intellectual development. According to Brooks, "[My father] was my first and most brilliant professor, and he taught me the meaning of words, of intellectual power, African-American history, literature, and culture. He recognized the critical importance of how black people in particular might use language as a tool for transformation. . . . He and my mom gave me the courage to write, to dream, to imagine." She adds, "I know that my voice as a scholar and as a writer is that of my father's. Daddy always encouraged me to make my voice heard, to use my voice and my love of writing as an instrument for change."[27] One reason why nurturing fathers tend to have the kinds of impact on their daughters that both Johnson and Brooks's fathers did on them is because they often offer their daughters a more open space to develop beyond traditional gender roles. For example, Coltrane notes that traditional fathers "tend to sex-type their children, overstimulate infants, and engage in rough and tumble play," and "caretaking fathers tend to interact verbally with their children, allow for self-direction, and treat sons and daughters similarly."[28] Indeed my wife often blames Misha's verbosity on me: too many lectures attended, too many interviews overheard, and too many complex ruminations on the most simplistic of things. And I'd be lying if I didn't admit that I do want to recreate myself in my daughter, encouraging her love of words, art, music, and creativity.

Black men seeing themselves as nurturing fathers is only the beginning of a process in which a black feminist fatherhood can be realized. Using Pruett's logic here, it's about black fathers seeing themselves as having something unique and important to offer to their daughters that will productively influence their lives as girls and later women, not just in terms of these girls developing a so-called masculine side, but in the very contexts in which they indeed see themselves as feminine. In many ways a black feminist fatherhood is about coming to terms with the lived experiences of black women and girls and imagining a world in which they can be empowered to be the kinds of women—people—they wish to be without the constraints of sexism, misogyny, homophobia, and racism. In one example, black comedian Aaron Freeman, who describes himself as a "feminist parent," writes, "No daughter of mine will ever file a sexual harassment suit. A guy who messes [with] my daughter will not pay for her lawyer, but his own doctor. I want my little girls to be bad bitches. I want them to terrorize all the little boys in the neighborhood"[29] Although I might distance myself from the image that Freeman presents of his daughters inflicting terror on their male peers (this comes dangerously close to the very negative stereotypes of feminists circulating in the mainstream media), at its core Freeman's essay is about imagining the context in which his daughters can be personally empowered.

I share Freeman's desire to see my daughter Misha empowered to choose her own paths as a girl and woman. From the time she was born I sensed the importance of giving her the space to "roam" physically, emotionally, and intellectually often in the face of what some people might think of as conventional thinking. When Misha was a toddler, I often butted heads with my mother-in-law over my parenting style. With five grown children under her belt, my mother-in-law, who I often describe as the last American housewife, found an engaged and nurturing father a little strange. There were numerous times when my mother-in-law would complain privately to my wife that she wasn't sure that I knew what I was doing, citing her experiences as a mother, grandmother, and great-grandmother as evidence. For example, she never understood why my wife was so comfortable leaving Misha home with me during sick days or when my wife had to travel. Although my late father-in-law was supportive of his family he, like my father, saw his importance as being tied to his economic value to his family, thus it wasn't unusual that my mother-in-law didn't quite know what to do with her son-in-law. There were rarely "words" between us, but there were subtle moments, like when my mother-in-law once told Misha she was "acting like a boy." It was of course an innocuous statement, especially for a two-year-old, but representative of the simple challenges faced by parents trying to eradicate rigid gender roles in the lives of their children.

Part of my role as a so-called feminist father is to encourage Misha to do the kinds of things she wants (within reason) regardless of whether the larger society finds such things strange for a little girl. Nowhere has this been more explicit than with Misha's verbal skills. In this case I am not simply talking about her ability to express herself verbally, but her comfort in saying *anything* that reflects her desires and feelings at any given time, and admittedly it is something that my wife and I sometimes disagree about. My wife and I were both raised in families in which children just didn't get involved in "grown folks'" conversations. But in the spirit of a feminism that "speaks back," I've thought it important for Misha to indeed "speak back" to whatever, with the caveat that she remain respectful. I'd be lying if I said there were times when her ability to "speak back" hasn't been absolutely maddening and exasperating, but I also realize how well this will serve her as a young woman. Parke and Brott note the importance of such a strategy, stating that "Girls whose fathers play with them a lot, for example, tend to be more popular with their peers and more assertive in their interpersonal relationships throughout their lives." The researchers also cite further evidence that "extremely competent and successful women frequently recall their fathers as active and encouraging, playful and exciting."[30] Ironically both my wife and my mother-in-law possess sarcastic wits that suggest that they too understand the importance of women being able to "speak back" to the world.

But even as I pursue the idea of a black feminist fatherhood, I admittedly am driven by the very issues that drive most responsible fathers, like the examples of my father and late father-in-law. Thus there are so many moments where I am literally frozen by the fear of not being able to provide economically for my family. Though I make a fairly comfortable living as a writer and academic (most comfortable because of my flexible schedule) my fear of not providing, in collaboration with the "over-achiever" in me, often means I have to struggle mightily with the tensions of being "on my grind" and being a feminist daddy. According to Silverstein, this tension "addresses one of the paradoxes of patriarchal society in that although fathers have had enormous economic power over their children, they have remained emotionally isolated from the intimate relationships of family life."[31] I still struggle with this notion of intimacy with my daughter and wife, though my ability to come to terms with its importance has manifested itself in my hyper-awareness of my mortality. That same fear of not being able to provide for my family is often expressed in the fear of dying suddenly and not being around for my family, particularly my daughter. As for so many Americans, the tragedy of September 11, 2001 was a reminder of just how fleeting life can be. Some of my most cherished memories of being a father are of trying to protect Misha from any knowledge of the attacks and any knowledge that the world she would grow up in had changed in serious and fundamental ways. In this way, my fears underlie an urgency that I now feel as a father, which often manifest themselves in a commitment to creating moments where I can truly be that engaged, nurturing, and yes, feminist father.

And yet there's still that small part of me that can't help but think about Misha as simply "daddy's little girl," something that I'm reminded of when I break down in tears, virtually every time I hear Johnny Hartman's vocal rendition of Bill Evans's "Waltz for Debby": "In her own sweet world/populated by dolls and clowns and a prince and a big purple bear/lives my favorite girl,

unaware of worried frowns that we weary grownups all wear."
Ironically Misha came to a sense of feminism on her own, courtesy of a Disney Channel production, of all things. *Cheetah
Girls* was based on a series of "tween" novels written by journalist Deborah Gregory that focus on five teenage girls of color
who live in New York City. The film featured Raven (Symone)
and singing group 3LW members Adrienne Bailon and Kiely
Williams. "Girl Power" and "Cinderella" were two of the songs
featured on the film's soundtrack. The former celebrated the
potential of little brown girls ("throw your hands up/if you know
that you're a star"), but it was the explicitly feminist "Cinderella"
that captivated Misha. Taking aim at *Cinderella*, one of the defining myths of childhood femininity, the Cheetah Girls defiantly
state that they don't want to be like Cinderella, coyly singing,
"I can slay my own dragons . . . my knight in shining armor is
me," and I thought it was such a wonderful sentiment to pass
on to little girls in a world that encourages them from the time of
their birth to seek out a male protector and provider, whether
Prince Charming or the baby-daddy around the way. As I rum-
maged through Misha's CD collection one day trying to find her
Cheetah Girls CD, she asked why I was looking for it and before
I could answer she said, "I know you want to listen to it, Daddy,
because it's cool." I couldn't help thinking to myself, "Yes, baby-
girl, brown girl feminism is cool."

In her essay "Fathering is a Feminist Issue" Silverstein makes
explicit connections between fatherhood and feminism, suggesting that "redefining fathering to reflect a primary emphasis
on nurturing and caretaking, as well as providing, is the next
necessary phase in the continuing feminist transformation of
patriarchal culture for the benefit of women as well as men."[32]
Silverstein's assertion became most clear to me when my role
as a nurturing father—a feminist father—ran into conflict with
my career as a music journalist. For some time I had been a
strong supporter of R&B vocalist R. Kelly, arguing in my book
Soul Babies: Black Popular Culture and the Post-Soul Aesthetic

that the artist often functioned in the role of a social critic who "provides meaningful critiques of contemporary black life."[33] But I had to re-evaluate my relationship to Kelly and his music when he was indicted on twenty-one counts of child pornography in June of 2002.[34] Six months later an additional twelve counts were added. A month after the last set of indictments, Kelly released his sixth CD, *The Chocolate Factory.* Thinking about reviewing the CD for one of the publications I wrote for, I couldn't help but think that such a review would make me a criminal or rather a "critical" accomplice.

The indictments against Kelly stem from a series of widely distributed videotapes in which he is purported to have sex with young girls as young as thirteen-years old. Throughout his career, R. Kelly has been haunted by rumors of his rapturous relations with underage girls. His brief marriage to the late Aaliyah in 1994 (she was fifteen at the time) was just the most visible proof of those rumors. In late 2000, allegations against Kelly became public as two different women alleged that the adult Kelly had sex with them when they were minors. Both women were students at Kenwood Academy in Hyde Park, which Kelly also attended as a teen. Kelly settled a suit with another accuser in 1998.[35] By the time the videotape emerged in February of 2002—on the eve of Kelly's performance at the opening ceremonies of the Salt Lake City Olympics—a clear pattern had emerged: R. Kelly was likely a pedophile and a child pornographer. In response to the indictments, folk went into celebrity surveillance mode, as Kelly's music, movements, and mediated messages were subject to intense scrutiny. Many urban radio outlets were at the center of the frenetic coverage as program directors (PDs) were faced with decisions over whether to continue to play Kelly's music. When stories about Kelly's problems surfaced in 2000, Todd Cavanah, the PD at Chicago's WBBM-FM, admitted that "We play hit songs from hit artists that our audience likes, and R. Kelly is one of them."[36] Cavanah's tone was very different when Kelly was indicted two years later and he decided to pull Kelly's music from his station's playlist: "Now that it's a real case, with a grand jury indictment, it's a serious issue. . . . We have community standards to live up to, and this is the right thing to do." In contrast, Marv Dyson, the general manager at WGCI-FM, also in Chicago, offered that "He's innocent until proven guilty. . . . At this moment our plan is to continue playing his music."[37]

When bootlegged videos of R. Kelly Exposed began to appear on the streets of major cities and various links to the "R. Kelly sex video" began to circulate throughout the Internet, it was clear that folks were more interested in the R. Kelly angle than the well-being of the young girl(s) in the video. Seemingly lost in the exchange of dollars and Internet links was the fact that those folks who sold and bought R. Kelly Exposed or who forwarded and opened Internet links, was the fact that they too were trafficking in child pornography. Such oversights are likely to occur within a culture that valued Kelly's celebrity over the lives of the young *black* girls who accused him of having sexual contact with them. The issue of race was easily glossed over in much of the coverage of Kelly's sexcapades. Mary Mitchell was one of the few commentators who addressed the significance of the racial identity of the girls, writing, "As long as [Kelly] is being accused of having sex with underage black girls, the allegations will draw a collective yawn." In contrast she writes, "What would have happened had Kelly gone to an affluent area like Naperville or Winnetka to recruit choir girls . . . had Kelly been accused of touching a golden hair on just one girl's head, he would have been put under the jail."[38]

And this was part of the irony that I considered as I began to write about R. Kelly's *The Chocolate Factory*. What if Kelly had been Justin Timberlake or Eminem? Would the conversation fall back so easily into one where a white man mistreated and exploited (raped?) a young black girl because of his racist views of black women? And of course it *did* when Benzino (Ray Scott), a marginal hip-hop artist and part owner of the now defunct magazine *The Source* tried to incite black audiences to speak out against Eminem (Marshall Mathers) when a tape that the white rapper made when he was a teenager was unearthed. On the tape he "dissed" black girls by referring to them as "dumb."[39] Pearl Cleage addressed such a reality in *Mad at Miles* as she wondered "what if Kenny [G] was revealed to be kicking black men's asses all over the country . . . what if Kenny [G] wrote a book saying that sometimes he had to slap black men around a little just to make them cool out and leave him the fuck alone."[40] For Cleage, the idea that black folks would close ranks around folks who harmed other black folks is unconscionable, be those folks black or white. Not surprisingly, R. Kelly's *Chocolate Factory* sold over 550,000 copies in its first week, making it the number one recording on the Soundscan chart for the week.

As a longtime fan of Kelly's music I was one of those who purchased the recording. Three of the songs on *Chocolate Factory* were originally slated for *Loveland*. The latter recording was scrapped because of bootlegging. I was forwarded a bootlegged copy of *Loveland* in early 2002 and listened to it quite regularly as it was the most mature and sophisticated music of Kelly's career. A favorite of mine was the original version of the song "Step in the Name of Love," a tribute to the stepper-set culture of Kelly's native Chicago. As innocuous as Kelly's "I Believe I Can Fly" or the "Electric Slide," the song quickly became a favorite of Misha's and very often the two of us could be heard chanting "Step, step, side to side, round and round, dip it now, separate, bring it back, let me see you do the love slide" while bumping down the highway in the car. But one day when Misha asked to hear the song again, it finally struck me that if she was ten years older I wouldn't even want her in the same room with R. Kelly. Suddenly it became clear to me that a figure like Kelly posed a threat not only to my daughter, but a host of other daughters. In the aftermath of the disturbing commercial success of Kelly's *Chocolate Factory* (in which

I'm admittedly implicated), there were even more disturbing moments like when Kelly stood in front of the audience at the BET Awards in June of 2003 to acknowledge the importance of "black folk standing up for each other" as if trying to protect young black girls from pedophiles and other sexual predators is not about standing up for black folk.

No doubt R. Kelly's incredible level of productivity in the aftermath of his indictments has been motivated by escalating legal expenses and calculated payoffs to the families of women who *could* be called to testify against him in a court of law. There's something terribly insidious about listening to R. Kelly floss about being the "Pied Piper of R&B." For whatever reasons, audiences seem to gravitate toward the man's worst (and least artistic) impulses. So tracks like "The Snake" and "Thoia Thoinga" (from his greatest hits package *The R in R&B*), which folk treated as if it was the new jump-off, represent so little of the genius that Kelly is capable of, genius that was powerfully evident on the bootlegged *Loveland*. But paying close attention to the fable that Kelly attaches himself to, folks seem to forget that the piper took off with the town's kids when they didn't pay up for his getting rid of the rats. And let's be straight: R. Kelly is making off with our kids, but not necessarily as the thirty-something man-child eyeballing your fourteen-year-old in the plaid skirt, but rather as the songwriter and producer of the little shorties that your kids swear are the second coming.

What has made R. Kelly peerless over the last twelve years are his abilities as a recording artist, songwriter, arranger, and producer. Ten years ago it was the late Aaliyah and Changing Faces, most recently it's been The Isley Brothers and Ginuwine, but today Kelly is reproducing himself right at the center of black kiddie pop, working with acts like the now defunct B2K, Marques Houston, Cassidy, Nick Cannon, JS (The Johnson Sisters), and Nivea. Kelly got into the mix with B2K on the group's second disc, *Pandemonium*, producing the track "Bump, Bump, Bump." He also produced the song "Girlfriend," one of the additional tracks on the deluxe upgrade of *Pandemonium*, that was released in March of 2003. Kelly wisely chose not to appear in many of these videos including that for Nivea's "Laundromat," though he does in fact sing opposite her on the song. A man accused of inappropriate sexual behavior with minors obviously can't show up in a music video cooing in the ear of a teenager. Kelly's stand-in for the "Laundromat" video was Nick Cannon, of the films *Drumline* and *Love Don't Cost a Thing* and long-time veteran of the Nickelodeon channel. Like Britney Spears before him and Hillary Duff currently, Cannon is trying to translate kiddie fame into a sustainable career. As a label-mate (both Cannon and Kelly record for Jive), Kelly was more than willing to lend a hand and in fact cast Cannon as the DJ in the video for his song "Ignition (remix)." Perhaps feeling his oats and no doubt feeling all the love pouring from the folk up in the balcony (a metaphor for those folks who don't care who you molested, but still want to get down), Kelly is very present in Cannon's video "Feeling Freaky" which also featured B2K.

I was in the living room one evening watching the Nickelodeon channel with Misha, when Nick Cannon's image came across the screen. As my daughter yelped, "Look, Daddy, it's Nick Cannon!" I thought about the fact that if she were ten or eleven years old, I probably would have had to take her to the *Scream III* tour that Cannon, B2K, and Marques Houston were headlining during the summer of 2003. But there is indeed something to consider when the music performed at a major kiddie pop tour featured music written and produced by a man accused of sexual relations with underage women. The Pied Piper indeed.

Four-year-old Misha Gabrielle was with my wife and me the day after Thanksgiving in 2002 as we sat in a local restaurant. It was our first time "out" since we heard that we would not be adopting a second child. Symbolically the day out was an acknowledgment on the part of my wife and me that we were finally moving on from a very painful and disappointing situation. It was while sitting there, as we thought about using the money we set aside for the adoption to plan a trip to Disney World, that we got the call on my cell phone from our lawyer letting us know that the birth-mother had again changed her mind and decided to go ahead with the adoption. Camille Monet has been with us since December 2002 (a day before my birthday). These days my notions about my masculinity are firmly tied to how good a parent I am to my two daughters. Despite my hang-ups initially about having a new baby in the house, fatherhood has been a breeze the second time around and I'm more confident than ever in my skills as a father and co-nurturer. It is me who now asks my wife, "When are we going to adopt the next one?" I'm in a house full of women and I'm thinking it's time to bring a little boy into the mix, if only so that there'll be another black boy in the world who will grow up to become an engaged, nurturing, feminist father.

Chapter 5

"ms. fat booty" and the black male feminist

"Ass so phat you can see it from the front?" Damn that must be some ass. "Ms. Fat Booty" was the lead single from hip-hop artist Mos Def's solo debut *Black on Both Sides* (1999). Mos Def had been firmly established as one of hip-hop's next generation of "conscious" soothsayers on the basis of *Mos Def and Talib Present Black Star,* his politically sophisticated collaboration with Talib Kweli. Despite his reputation as one of the most *conscious* of conscious hip-hop artists, the song remains one of his most well-known tracks and one of the songs that regularly gets mentioned in the context of conversations around the sexism and misogyny that circulates throughout much of hip-hop culture. The meaning and value of songs like "Ms. Fat Booty" can easily be misinterpreted. Is the song the product of a sexist culture that objectifies the bodies of black women? Or is "Ms. Booty" a celebration, a tribute to black femininity in the context of a larger society that often denigrates the beauty and physical attributes of black women? "Ms. Fat Booty" also happens to be one of my favorite Mos Def songs if not one of my favorite hip-hop songs period.

And there's the quandary: Black male writer and scholar, on the frontline with other brothers of all walks of life, who view themselves, not just as fellow travelers of the black feminist movement, but as feminists in their own right. Do feminists check out each other's asses? We know the asses "conscious" black male rappers check out, but how about black male feminists? My affection for Mos Def's "Ms. Fat Booty" frames one of the contradictions of thinking oneself a black male feminist. For example, how does black male feminism deal with the reality of heterosexual desire? I've consciously looked at more than a few asses like the one Mos Def describes. Or how does this black male feminist explain the aural pleasure he derives from hearing Snoop Dogg's flow on the remix of 50 Cent's "P.I.M.P."?—"Yeah girl I got my Now and Later gators on"— a song whose music video features the very kinds of images that I speak out against as scholar and critic. To speak out against the gratuitous vulgarities of hip-hop is the easy part. The difficulty comes in trying to do so while still affirming the aesthetic and cultural value of hip-hop at the same time. Too often those ready and willing to do the former are ill equipped to do the latter.

As a card-carrying member of hip-hop generation (in the game since 1978), someone whose political, social, and cultural consciousness has, in part, been shaped by the music, the culture, and the icons of hip-hop, I am well aware of the sexist, misogynistic, and homophobic tendencies among some of the genre's purveyors and supporters. And although I've never bought into hip-hop's visceral violence—both literal and rhetorical—and the pleasures derived from that violence, my embrace of hip-hop is obviously complicated by my desire to embody the ideals of black male feminism. This seeming contradiction became quite

clear to me a few years ago while attending an academic conference in Hartford, Connecticut. Having spent the day attending
panel discussions, I hopped in the rental car looking to find
someplace to grab a bite to eat. While waiting at a stoplight, the
local "urban" station put on The Notorious B.I.G.'s "Dreams."
It's a song I hadn't heard in quite some time and quite honestly
is one of the late rapper's best performances, so of course I
rolled down the windows and turned up the volume. In the
song Biggie describes (all too vividly) his sexual attraction to
about twenty-five female R&B singers and rappers, including
a then-fifty-year-old Patti Labelle. So as I'm sitting at the
light, doing the requisite hip-hop head nod while Biggie coos
"dreams of fuckin' an R&B bitch," Angela Davis—yes *that*
Angela Davis—comes strolling across the street. I do not know
Ms. Davis, but I'm very familiar with her scholarship and legacy as an activist. As I quickly turned down the radio and hit
the gas pedal as the light changed, I imagined finally being
introduced to Ms. Davis one day, her calling me out, and me
having to fall back into that "Well what had happened" mode
that seems synonymous with black male explanations for various public transgressions. OJ Simpson, Kobe Bryant, and Jesse
Jackson have all done some version of this. Since that incident
at the stoplight, I knew it would be important for me to explore
with some detail the contradictions of being a fan and supporter of all forms of hip-hop (Jay Z has been my scholarly and
creative muse for the last five years, for example) and a black
male feminist.

For much of its sojourn on planet America, hip-hop has
been a primary site for the articulation of distinct forms of
black masculinity: urban, hyper-masculine, hyper-sexual, pseudo-
criminalized. Included among those expressions of black masculinity have been often contradictory and even competing
ideals about women, in particular black women. In a world best
described as having a "bitch/queen" complex, where a figure
like the late Tupac Shakur could wax poetically about sexually

exploiting women ("I Get Around" and "Hit 'Em Up") and find a real spiritual grounding with the "round-the-way" girl in songs like "Brenda's Got a Baby" and "Keep Your Head Up," there are clear contradictions associated with the issue of gender and sexuality. Tupac is just the most well-known case of a seeming schizophrenia that articulates a real fear and distrust of black femininity (like the group Bell Biv Devoe expressed so well years ago with "Never Trust a Big Butt and a Smile") and a real passion for those black women who adhere to traditional notions of femininity that allow for unfettered visions of black masculinity, whether it is Akinyele's wishing for a "six foot blow-job machine" (in reference to his many songs about such things) or Common getting misty-eyed thinking about his grandmother on the track "Payback is a Grandmother."

But to see tracks like Mos Def's "Ms. Fat Booty" or Sir Mix-o-Lot's "Baby Got Back" simply as efforts to objectify black women, is to miss the point of the productive ways that young black men celebrate black female physicality, in the context of a culture that holds certain versions of white femininity (willowy and wispy) as the ideal beauty standard for American society, if not the world. Thus lines like "Ass so phat you can see it to the front" or "I like big butts!" although visually tied to some of the most widely circulated stereotypes about black women (can the Hottentot Venus get some love up in here?), are efforts by figures like Mos Def and Sir Mix-o-Lot to give praise to the uniqueness of black femininity. One man's celebration can easily become the other man's objectification, and very often it is difficult to reconcile legitimate critiques of hip-hop as being sexist and misogynistic and equally legitimate attempts by black male hip-hop artists to give love to the beauty and diversity of black women's bodies and quite frankly, to give voice to the pleasures they derive from those bodies.

In the context of contemporary black life and culture, accusations of sexism and misogyny in the lyrics and music videos of hip-hop artists are often the only times that those issues get discussed, at least publicly. Periodically there are instances when a particular song or image heightens the focus on sexism and misogyny within the black community, though most often that focus rarely extends beyond an examination of hip-hop. More than a decade ago C. Delores Tucker mounted one of the largest campaigns to address the vulgarity that circulates within hip-hop. In late 1993 Tucker threw the weight of the National Political Congress of Black Women (NPCBW), an organization she helped found in 1985, behind a petition drive which aimed to pressure record companies that trafficked in so-called "gangsta rap." At the time Tucker stated that "Our nation cannot be whole if we permit the continuation of an art form that teaches children that rape, hate and disrespect are OK, and threatens the safety of our communities."[1] The Time Warner corporation and its subsidiary Interscope Records became Tucker's most well-known target. Interscope distributed Death Row Records, which at the time featured former N.W.A. member Dr. Dre and his protégé Snoop Dogg, whose debut album for the label became the first ever by a new artist to top the pop charts upon release. Among Tucker's strategies was to buy stock in record store chains like The Wiz and Musicland and corporate entities like Sony and Time Warner just so she could use shareholder meetings as a forum for her complaints.[2] Ultimately her efforts forced Time Warner to sell the company's fifty percent stake in Interscope back to the label's founders Ted Field and Jimmy Iovine.[3]

For several reasons Tucker's efforts had a limited impact on hip-hop audiences and ultimately the music that was created. Most notable was Tucker's seemingly bizarre alliance with conservative pundit and Republican Party stalwart William Bennett in the mid-1990s. Tucker has a history of left activism, at least as framed by the traditional civil rights movement, but she quite comfortably fell in with Bennett in an attempt to censure the recording industry, though she admitted, "We may disagree on politics, but when it comes to children we are together."[4] As journalist Bakari Kitwana keenly observed at the time, "Tucker is someone who's committed to what's going on in the black community. . . . But Bill Bennett and Bob Dole, they just say 'rap is bad' without ever listening to the music." Further, Kitwana noted that the criticism of rap is often "done in a way that is not that different from the way George Bush used Willie Horton in the 1988 campaign," making reference to a series of Republican ads.[5] Horton was a convicted felon who committed murder after being released on a furlough program in the state of Massachusetts.[6] Ironically the very criticisms that Kitwana makes of Bennett and Dole, who made anti-rap rhetoric part of his 1996 presidential campaign, could easily be applied to Tucker also as there is little evidence that as a nearly seventy-year-old woman, she had any clear sense of the context in which hip-hop was created and circulated within black youth culture.

Most recently campaigns have been mounted within the black community over the circulation of the term "pimp" within hip-hop culture. The specific impetuses for these campaigns were the song "P.I.M.P." by 50 Cent, particularly a live performance of the song on MTV in which young women of color appeared wearing dog collars and leashes, and a sports drink marketed by rap act Nelly and named after his song "Pimp Juice." Always a barometer of the civil rights generation's disdain for the hip-hop generation, noted curmudgeon Stanley Crouch chimed, "Black popular culture continues to descend. The most recent and monstrous aspect of it comes, as usual from the world of hip-hop," adding, "This new development is observable in . . . the elevation of pimps as cultural heroes. That's beyond degraded."[7] In another example, a Columbus, Ohio resident wrote, "Don't blacks have to deal with enough negative stereotypes daily and in the media? Don't we, as black people, get tired of this? Again, let's be honest: We can't blame whites for this one, can we?"[8]

Many of the youngest of the hip-hop generation were not privy to 1970s television dramas like *Starsky & Hutch* and *Kojak* or films like *The Mack* and *Superfly*, where black male pimps were staple characters. Antonio Fargas, who played "Huggy Bear" on *Starsky and Hutch*, may have been the most recognizable "pimp" in America during the 1970s. Some of the older cats can remember reading the fiction of Robert Beck (Iceberg Slim) whose autobiography *Pimp: The Story of My Life* was required reading for wannabe playas in the 1970s. Others might remember reading the stories of Donald Goines, who after being inspired by Iceberg Slim's confessional, wrote a series of "urban" novels in which pimps were often seminal figures. As John Robinson notes in *The Guardian*, for Slim the pimp game was "seldom about violence to women. It was all about verbal persuasion. Even, controversially charm."[9] Noted historian Robin D.G. Kelley made a similar observation a few years ago in a controversial *New York Times* article about Miles Davis. In the piece Kelley suggested that the legendary jazz artist was a product of the "pimp aesthetic . . . a masculine culture that aspired to be like a pimp, that embraced the cool performative styles of the players (pronounced 'playa'), the 'macks,' the hustlers, who not only circulated in the jazz world but whose walk and talk also drew from the well of black music."[10] As Snoop Dogg reflected, "We're teaching people how to hustle and how to look good. . . . I'd rather be a pimp than a gang-banger, because I grew up a gang-banger, and I'll tell you, you live longer being a pimp."[11]

Hip-hop's fascination with the pimp aesthetic dates back to the release of *Hustler's Convention* (1973), a recording from former Last Poet Jalal Nuriddin, who used the name Lightnin' Rod for the album. Closer in style to the spoken word flow of the Black Arts Movement than what we think of as hip-hop, nevertheless tracks like "Four Bitches Is What I Got" and "Coppin' Some Fronts for the Sets" became the linguistic building blocks for the next generation of wannabe players. Hip-hop artists like Big Daddy Kane ("Pimpin' Ain't Easy"), Ice T (allegedly a former pimp), and Too Short, in particular, are singular influences on the pimp aesthetic within contemporary hip-hop culture. But for some hip-hop generation audiences, pimps were little more than cartoonish characters in music videos like Snoop's "Doggy Dog World" or figures that Snoop, Too Short, and others nostalgically paid tribute to with shoulder-length perms, big-ass Cadillacs, and "Now-and-Later" gators. Pimps gained new credibility within hip-hop recently on the strength of Jay Z's crossover hit "Big Pimpin'" (2000) and 50 Cent's "P.I.M.P." remix which also featured a cameo by Bishop Don "Magic" Juan, the chairman of the board of the Famous Players Association, sponsors of the legendary Players Ball. The Bishop has become a literal celebrity on the strength of his popularity within hip-hop circles, including a star turn in the documentary *American Pimp* (2000). Purportedly one of the most notorious pimps in the country in the early 1980s, Bishop Don Juan apparently had a spiritual conversion in 1985 and "gave up the game" (though he apparently kept his pimp style) for the pulpit.[12]

When the Bishop's Players Ball came to Atlanta in 2001, a video of the event was taped as part of a child prostitution investigation in the city.[13] Two years later when the Ball came to Atlanta during the National Basketball Association's (NBA) All-Star Weekend, it was targeted for protest under the pretext that there was a connection between the Ball and the child prostitution ring in the city. But the event's promoter Lisa Thomas was quick to respond that "There will not be any children, any prostitution, any pimps, anyone selling anybody at all. . . . This is just a party."[14] This particular view of The Players Ball was corroborated by photographers Coreen and Suzanne Simpson who were invited to one of the balls in Chicago and describe the vibe at the event as "cocktail-partyish, even laid back at times."[15] In many ways the Players Ball is an infomercial that soft pedals pimp-style without dealing with the intricacies of the pimp-game. As the Bishop put it, pimping has been "portrayed negatively through movies and television. . . . Now people are seeing it for what it is."[16] It's the ultimate hustle, a hustle predicated on *the* hustle or as writer Beth Coleman describes it, an example of the pimp's ability to "exploit exploitation" and therein lies part of the appeal of the pimp to the hip-hop generation.[17] According to scholar Eithne Quinn, "The pimp constitutes an icon of upward mobility for black working-class males, spectacularly refusing, through their heightened style politics, the subservient type-casting that has historically been imposed by the dominant social order." Making a link between hip-hop artists and pimps, Quinn notes that the "mythic pimp, like the rapper, is able to convert subcultural capital into economic capital."[18] The success of a post-pimping Bishop Don "Magic" Juan may be the best example of this phenomenon. As Quinn further observes, "The resurgence of pimp culture signals a deep material and symbolic investment in life style and leisure pursuits, which accompanies economic and employment frustration."[19]

Quinn also places the new cachet of the pimp in the context of changing gender relationships within black communities. Quinn suggests that "Shifting gender roles and relations, fostered in part by the diminishing job opportunities for blue-collar men, may have something to do with the black hustling imagination . . . alighting on the misogynists and extremely patriarchal pimp figure."[20] Quinn's observation creates a context to examine the dual roles of a figure like Snoop Dogg, who while benefiting from a metaphoric connection to pimping—Bishop Don "Magic" Juan is his spiritual advisor—is clearly invested in the exploitation of women. For example, in an attempt to distance himself from traditional notions of "pimping" as violent, Snoop Dogg argues that folk "just think it's take money from a girl and slap her and send her to the corner, but nah it's other things . . . the freedom of the females and the thought of a female getting' you money."[21] Although Snoop Dogg surely has creative and metaphoric license to imagine a world where women are providers, his musings have concrete implications when one considers his role as host of the soft porn video series *Girls Gone Wild*. In a show of race pride, Snoop Dogg quit his role as host over the lack of women of color in the series. He told the Associated Press back in 2003, "If you notice, there hasn't been no girls of (ethnicity) at all on none of those tapes. . . . No black girls, no Spanish girls—all white girls, and that (stuff) ain't cool, because white girls ain't the only hos that get wild."[22] Are Snoop Dogg's comments representative of somebody who exploits black women or are his comments in some bizarre way a loving expression of black female sexuality?

When the happy-go-lucky rapper Nelly decided to tap into the pimp aesthetic on *Nellyville* (2002), the follow-up to his debut *Country Grammar*, which sold close to ten million copies, he was likely calculating that his arguably white-bread pop image would withstand and likely be emboldened by such a move. Now, I'll be the first to admit that I cringed the first time I heard Nelly's song "Pimp Juice," it was an automatic reaction to Nelly's attempt at a pimp-styled falsetto (see Paul Wingfield's "18 with a Bullet" for the definitive example) and the fact he would name anything Pimp Juice without even a hint of irony. But "Pimp Juice" was also the name of an energy drink that Nelly threw his name behind. Pimp Juice, the energy drink, was a joint venture between Nelly and the Fillmore Street Brewing Company, based in Nelly's hometown of St. Louis, Missouri. The drink was described as "non-carbonated energy atypical to the usual soda-like energy drinks. It consists of 10 percent apple juice, with 100 percent of vitamins C, B-6, B-12. riboflavin, niacin and pantothenic acid."[23] Despite its rather innocuous description, Pimp Juice arguably became the most controversial energy drink ever.

Groups like Project Islamic Hope, the National Alliance for Positive Action, and the National Black Anti-Defamation League, along with ministers Michael Pfleger and Paul Scott quickly called for a national black boycott of Pimp Juice. According to

Najee Ali of Project Islamic Hope, "We intend to chase Nelly's *Pimp Juice* out of the black community."[24] Minister Scott added from his Durham, North Carolina base, "As black men we should be building a nation of strong black leaders, not a nation of super energized, drunk pimps."[25] Columnist Clarence Page chimed in that "Back in the prehistoric age before there was rap music or, for that matter, laptops or cell phones, my generation had such terms as 'pimp walk,' 'pimp style,' or simply 'pimpin' some sucker who didn't know any better. But we never had any confusion as to where the word came from."[26] Page's comments get to the heart of the controversy, as this is another example of how much distance there is between the civil rights old guard and the hip-hop generation. Whereas the old guard can only see literal pimps, many within the hip-hop generation have redefined the word to suit the needs of the post–civil-rights era world.

In response to old-guard concerns, noted public intellectual Michael Eric Dyson suggested, "For those who are mad literalists it would be problematic to defend and justify a practice whereby women are exploited. But [pimping] has been seen more in its metaphoric intensity; that is to say it's an analogy for how black men who are on the underside of society catch on, get over and engage in practices that may be seen outside of traditional orthodox society and yet allows them to get over."[27] Although the word still clearly alludes to the practice of exploitation, it is no longer solely rooted in some archaic notion of "pimps up, ho's down." As Nelly cogently described to Sylvester Brown, Jr. in the *St. Louis Post-Dispatch,* "What we have been able to do in hip-hop is to take a negative and turn it into a positive . . . . if you pimp something, that means you're getting the most out of the best of you ability."[28] This sentiment was expressed a year before the Pimp Juice controversy when organizers of the *Pimp Harder* fashion show during the homecoming celebration at Howard University responded to accusations that they were normalizing pathological behavior. According to organizers Jessica Lima and Megan Moore, they hoped the show would inspire Howard students to "conquer what oppresses them and become pimps in their own right." For these women the word "pimp" can even be applied to feminist sensibilities. As Moore asserts, "pimping is a state of mind . . . a movement about no longer being the victim, a movement where women do not have to take some of the crap that men dish out."29

Generally speaking we all understand that literal pimps have been some of the most nefarious characters to ever languish (it's not like they're thriving) within black communities, finding power and notoriety (and at times celebrity) in their exploitation and often violent control of black female sexuality. But in many regards the bad and justifiable reputation that pimps have endured has been a smokescreen to mask the equally nefarious exploitative habits of those within more "respectable" black institutions. Chicago-based hip-hop artist Common alluded to such in his song "A Film Called Pimp" (2000), as he gives up the "game" telling his would-be "ho," well "Fuck you then, I'm about to be a preacher." Although the Chi-town native may have been shouting out fellow Chi-town playa Bishop Don "Magic" Juan, there's no small irony in the fact that the very skills and tools that make an effective pimp—language, style, charisma, manipulation—are often desired and valued by men of the cloth. Thus I must question the motivation of a group like Project Islamic Hope, which has been at odds with the hip-hop generation since they lobbied against Tupac Shakur's nomination for an NAACP Image Award in the early 1990s. I wonder where Project Islamic Hope or the National Black Anti-Defamation League were when Gregory Love was beat-down in a homophobic attack in a Morehouse College bathroom and Sakia Gunn was stabbed to death in another homophobic attack. I wonder how come these groups haven't called for a boycott of R. Kelly records after his indictment on twenty-one charges of child pornography. Perhaps it's because said groups also understand the pimp game and they have successfully pimped the trivial and the inane in black life so they could do their own pimp strut for the national media.

Less than a year after the Pimp Juice controversy, Nelly was again embroiled in a controversy, this time involving the X-rated video for his song "Tip Drill." I've only seen the video once, but the few minutes of the video that I saw left an indelible image in my mind, that of a young African-American male running a credit card through the "crack" of a young black woman's "ass" as if it were a direct payment of some sort. The scholar in me found such an image "ironic"—black men essentially articulating their view of contemporary relations between the men and women of the hip-hop generation in an era of cash-and-carry sexual politics—the same irony that one might find in phrases like "chickenhead" and "bird" or a song like Nas's "You Owe Me." But taking seriously the world that my young daughters are charged with navigating, there was something disturbing and indeed frightening about the possibility of their being reduced to giant sexualized credit-card machines. Some of the young women at Spelman College, the historically black all-women's college in Atlanta, also found Nelly's "Tip Drill" video offensive.

Shortly after its release, the video piqued the interest of Moya Bailey, the president of Spelman College's Feminist Majority Leadership Alliance (FMLA). After sponsoring a viewing of the "Tip-Drill" video, followed by a discussion session, the organization voted to name Nelly the "Misogynist of the Month" in February of 2004.[30] Unbeknownst to Bailey and her organization, Nelly was to appear on the Spelman campus in April of 2004 in support of a bone marrow drive sponsored by his foundation *4Sho4Kids*. A few years ago Nelly began to raise consciousness about the need for more blood stem cell and bone marrow donors after his sister was diagnosed with leukemia. The Student Government Association (SGA) at Spelman had agreed to host the bone marrow drive months earlier, but after Asha

Jennings, president of the SGA, saw the "Tip-Drill" video on
BET's overnight video program *Uncut* and talked with Bailey,
she re-thought her organization's support of the event. According to Jennings, "Nelly wants us to help his sister . . . but he's
degrading hundreds of us," adding that "It was a moral issue. . . .
My integrity was on the line."[31] Jennings agreed to continue
support for the bone marrow drive with the added caveat that
Nelly also appear at a forum to discuss the portrayals of women
in hip-hop music videos. Nelly declined and in response to
planned protests, he and his foundation pulled out of the event.
Jennings later told the *Atlanta Journal-Constitution*, "We care
about the cause, and we understand the need for bone marrow
is so great within the minority community," but "We can't continue to support artists and images that exploit our women and
put us out there as over-sexed, non-intelligent human beings."[32]
As described by journalist and Spelman College professor
William Jelani Cobb, the decision to cancel the drive was "tantamount to saying 'shut up and give me your bone marrow.'"[33]

Responses to the Spelman protest ran the gamut, including
those who used the controversy as an opportunity to discuss
the finer points of what exactly a "tip-drill" is as if that was
really the point. Some detractors argued that the young women
at Spelman needed to get their priorities straight, suggesting that
the bone marrow drive was an issue more important than the
portrayal of women in hip-hop videos, videos that "many" of
the women at Spelman have supported in the past. For example, pop music critic Kevin Johnson wrote, "These ambitious
college students, while pursuing admirable goals, have decided
that taking Nelly to task for T&A videos is more important than
the health crisis bringing him to campus in the first place,"
adding that "It seems misguided to agree to host him for a
common good only to pull a bait and switch by introducing
an issue that's comparatively insignificant."[34] "Insignificant to
whom?" I'm apt to ask, but Johnson's comments do highlight
the fact that Nelly's "Tip-Drill" is just one of the most notorious

of the pornographic videos that appear regularly on BET's *Uncut*. Jennings is aware of such criticism admitting that "Our stand is not a heartless attack against Nelly, but it's opposition to the hip-hop culture we helped create by buying the music and supporting the videos."[35]

As with the example of Snoop Dogg's role in *Girls Gone Wild*, Nelly's "Tip-Drill" and BET's *Uncut* are further evidence of the increasingly common relationship between hip-hop culture and the pornography industry. It has become standard for many popular acts to shoot porn-style music videos for adult audiences and to make feature-length porn films. *Snoop Dogg's Doggystyle* (2001) was one of the first of the first full-length porn features that starred a mainstream hip-hop artist. Distributed by Larry Flynt's company, the video purportedly sold over a hundred thousand copies. Conscious of their role as mainstream spokespersons (Snoop, for example, hawks for Nokia and AOL), many mainstream rappers choose not appear onscreen in sexual acts, instead playing the role, as pop music critic Martin Edlund describes it, of "Master of ceremonies, presiding over the festivities."[36] Obviously such ventures are lucrative for both the artists and the porn industry. As one porn industry insider put it, "The fresh music brings people who are primarily fans of hip-hop to the adult genre. . . . We get a lot of customers that we might not otherwise get."[37]

BET's *Uncut* debuted in 2000 and is broadcast three nights a week at 3:00 A.M. (EST). BET has been under fire over the past few years for reducing their programming to soft-porn music videos. But *Uncut* takes it to another level. According to video director Nzingha Stewart, "It's almost like the other videos are like foreplay and the uncut videos are the act themselves." Speaking about the impact that videos like those shown on *Uncut* have on women, Stewart admits, "I don't think there should necessarily be censorship of the images of women, but it's an extremely one-sided look at women. There's no other images to counteract it. . . . I can't tell you the last video I saw where a black woman had a job, and that's really more our experience than black women being strippers."[38]

When BET founder Robert Johnson sold the network to Viacom in 2000, it was clear that Viacom valued BET for the distinctive content it provides. By 2000 that content was less about a distinct black point of view within mainstream media, but more so motivated by a desire on Viacom's part to control— exploit—the dominant provider of "urban" content on broadcast television. Journalist and feminist critic Joan Morgan, notes that in an earlier period, "MTV was besieged with complaints that its videos were too full of content inappropriate for younger kids." Highlighting the contradictions of Viacom (which also owns MTV) supporting a program like *Uncut*, Morgan asserts, "Evidently it wasn't acceptable to air near-pornographic images for the young, largely White audiences of MTV, but it was fine to dump them on the young, largely Black BET audience."[39] If we take seriously William Jelani Cobb's observations that videos like "Tip Drill" and Ludacris's "Booty Poppin'" are "part of a centuries-long debasement of black women's bodies" and "hip hop artists' verbal and visual renderings of black women are now virtually indistinguishable from those of 19th century white slave owners," then we can also take seriously the fact that Johnson and Viacom CEO Mel Karmazin have "pimp game" that's "way stronger" than any Snoop or 50 Cent could concoct.[40]

In the context of Nelly's "Tip-Drill" video, women are only good for one thing, and even then, only from the back. "Tip-Drill" is representative of a world where young black men often view young black women as "chickenheads," "skeezers," "gold-diggers," "birds," and a host of other unsavory adjectives. The common denominators are that such women are viewed as being solely motivated by their desire for money and are only valued as sex objects, hence the highlighting of cash-and-carry sexual relationships. In many ways "Tip-Drill" is the logical follow-up to "You Owe Me," Nas's club hit from 2000. The song, which was produced by Timbaland and features vocals by Ginuwine, drops gems like "Yeah, owe me back like you owe your tax/Owe me back like forty acres to Blacks." The latter lyric incredibly equates Nas's "getting some ass" with reparations for the descendants of enslaved Africans. On the recent DVD release of the *Nas Video Anthology Volume 1*, the artist quips that he simply wanted a "club hit."

The seemingly widespread belief by some young black men that young black women are wholly motivated by economics in the pursuit of heterosexual relationships informed some critics of the Spelman protest. These critics were quick to note that many of the women who appear in videos like "Tip Drill" do so of their own accord and often free of charge. Male students from neighboring Morehouse College and Clark Atlanta University said things like, "These are grown women. I'm putting the blame on them" or "Bottom line, a black woman let him do that."[41] As one radio jock put it, the women in a video like "Tip-Drill" must "share the blame as much as the artists . . . if [rappers] say we want to swipe a credit card on your rear end, and all the young ladies say we're not going to do that, then they would cut the scene." For the record, "Tip-Drill" reportedly cost $80,000 to shoot and the women who *were* paid to appear in the video were paid between $200 and $2500. But the above comments neglect the economic realities of the porn industry, particularly as it relates to poor women of color. According to scholar Jayna Brown, "With welfare reform, we now see a resurgence of poor women of color turning to work in the sex industry . . . and given shrinking options in the current US domestic job market, sex work offers an alternative source of income." Brown adds that in the past, "We had the gangster, the killer, the drug dealer, but now it's the man who hustles in the sex industry. The emphasis has shifted from violence to sexual pleasure . . . When this is in the alternative of drugs and sex, [dollars] are usually made off of other black people's need to escape from the grim reality of imprisonment, poorly paying jobs and the lack of social services."[42]

Asha Jennings's concern with protecting her integrity and with doing something that was morally right could easily be read as an example of middle-class black women criticizing the images of the "Tip Drill" video in the name of protecting some sanitized view of black femininity. According to Moya Bailey, such criticism is valid: "As middle class, college educated black women, we can easily speak to the issue of video images, but the issue of financial barriers that lock women into being in these videos is not something that we seemed to address." She adds, "Our criticism was directed toward Nelly, not the women in his videos, but I do hope that to help them see that while they may feel autonomous in the choices they make, the implication of their decisions are global, impacting how African-American women are viewed world-wide."[43] Admittedly, not all of the women who show up in porn-style music videos could be described as impoverished and some even manage to make comfortable livings as so-called "video-hos." The reality though is that quite a few of these women take jobs appearing in videos like "Tip Drill" or Petey Pablo's "Freek-a-Leek" to augment the nearly minimum-wage salaries they make working during the day at some convenience store. But the theory that all of these women appear in *Uncut*-styled music videos for economic reasons also denies those women the ability to be seen as exhibiting sexual agency. In other words, arguments that suggest that women pursue music video "sex work" just for the money and even those arguments that suggest they are being exploited, potentially deny the possibility that these women are in fact in control of their own sexuality.

Noted black feminist critic and sociologist Patricia Hill-Collins makes such an observation in her book *Black Sexual Politics: African Americans, Gender, and the New Racism*. Writing about well-known "bootylicious" women through history—Sarah Bartmann ("Hottentot Venus"), Josephine Baker, Destiny's

Child, and Jennifer Lopez—Hill-Collins argues "Destiny's Child
may entertain and titillate; yet their self-definitions as 'survi-
vors' and 'independent women' express female power and celebration of the body and booty. . . . Their message contains a
defiance denied to Bartmann and Baker—'It's my body, it's my
booty, and I'll do what I want with it—can you handle it'?"[44]
Indeed with so much of the commentary about the "Tip-Drill"
focused on the act of that credit card being slid through that
woman's ass, little attention was paid to what *that* ass might
have been articulating. Hill-Collins's analysis asks us to consider *that* ass as part of an effort to "rescue and redefine sexuality as a source of power rooted in spirituality, expressiveness,
and love" that creates "new understandings of Black masculinity and Black femininity needed for a progressive Black sexual
politics."[45]

Hill-Collins introduces a level of complexity that is often
missing in discussions about hip-hop and black popular culture
in general, in relationship to black gender and sexual politics.
For most of hip-hop's thirty-something years, folk have been
compelled to point out the sexism, misogyny, and homophobia
that finds a forum in the lyrics of the young black and brown
men who have primarily influenced hip-hop, and the lack of a
womanist perspective that could directly counter those lyrics.
But I often wonder if it is possible that we are asking hip-hop,
particularly mainstream hip-hop, to do something that it is fundamentally incapable of doing. Let me be clear: I'm on the
front lines of any effort to get the men in hip-hop to rethink
their pornographic uses of women's bodies and performance of
lyrics that more often than not express, at best, a deep ambivalence about and fear of women and, at worst, outright hatred.
But as we make demands of these artists, we also must be clear
about what is happening within mainstream hip-hop. Without
doubt, the performance of black masculinity continues to be
the dominant creative force within hip-hop. As numbers have
shown fairly consistently over the last decade or so, young white

men are the primary consumers—at least in the traditional commercial sense—of the various performances of black masculinity and the pornographic images of black and brown women found in mainstream hip-hop.

By asking hip-hop to reform, we are essentially demanding the artists, record labels, and hip-hop's primary consumer base to produce and consume music that is anti-sexist, anti-misogynistic, and even feminist. In what context have young white men (or black men for that matter) ever been interested in consuming large amounts of black feminist thought? Clearly these young whites are consuming hip-hop for other reasons. In the case of young white males, hip-hop represents a space where they work through the idea of how their masculinity can be lived, that they literally take from the hyper-masculine "black buck" (think about Mr. Fiddy's influence in the killing fields of Iraq) and indeed it is an integral part of the cash-and-carry exchange.[46] In a society that remains largely ignorant of the scholarly, political, and cultural contributions of women such as Anna Julia Cooper, Audre Lorde, Angela Davis ("Oh yeah, she was the chick with the afro, right?"), June Jordan, bell hooks, Michele Wallace, Patricia Hill-Collins, Jewell Gomez, Joy James, Beverley Guy-Sheftall, and Masani Alexis De Veaux, how can we expect hip-hop to do the work that hasn't been done in the larger culture?

Despite popular belief, hip-hop is *not* the most prominent site of sexism and misogyny in American society but a reflection of the misogyny and sexism that more powerfully circulates within American culture. In many ways the images and lyrics used to objectify women of color in hip-hop videos serve as metaphors for the ways that American society actually treats those women. As critic Kevin Powell notes, "At its worst hiphop serves up some of the most destructive and myopic definitions of manhood this side of the caveman-like things Mick Jagger, Sid Vicious, and other drugged-up and oversexed rockers did and said," but cautions that "It is wrong to categorically dismiss

hiphop without taking into serious consideration the socioeco-
nomic conditions (and the many record labels that eagerly
exploit and benefit from the ignorance of many of these young
artists) that have led to the current state of affairs."[47] In her
book *Check it While I Wreck It: Black Womanhood, Hip-Hop
Culture and the Public Sphere*, scholar Gwendolyn Pough goes
a step further, arguing that "Rappers become grunt workers for
the patriarchy: they sow the field of misogyny for the patriarchy
and provide the labor necessary to keep it in operation, much as
Black men and women provided the free and exploited labor
that built the United States."[48] Remember, some of the black
men on the screen are "performing," performing their notions of
how American masculinity embodies power through force, violence, and exploitation. Mr. 50-Cent isn't the only thug or pimp
in the room; there are more than a few in the White House and
at the Pentagon.

In many ways, our discussions about hip-hop culture are the
product of a very myopic view of contemporary black expres-
sive culture. Yes, hip-hop needs to be reformed, but it's not as
if hip-hop is the only place where young black men and women
are discussing the very reasons why hip-hop remains so problematic to some of us. For example, Princeton University scholar
Daphne Brooks asserts that few critics have paid attention to
the significance of narratives by black female R&B artists. She
argues that "Black Women's popular desire is thus depoliticized
and disregarded for its reflections on domestic and socioeco-
nomic politics and sexual fulfillment." But she adds that what
"critics have failed to fully interrogate are the ways in which
this subgenre also operates as an extension of hip-hop culture
itself."[49] A good example of this is an artist like Syleena Johnson,
who has circulated within hip-hop via remixes with the Flip-
Mode Squad and most recently singing the "Lauryn Hill" hook
on Kanye West's "All Falls Down." On her disc *Chapter One:
Love, Pain and Forgiveness* (2001), Johnson recorded the track

"Hit on Me," which explicitly addressed the issue of domestic abuse.

If we think about contemporary black popular culture more broadly than what urban radio and BET tell us, then we are likely to find the work of artists like Ursula Rucker and Sarah Jones. Rucker first came to prominence performing spoken word poetry on The Roots' recordings *Do You Want More?!!!??!* (1995), *Illadelph Halflife* (1996) and *Things Fall Apart* (1999). In 2001 she released her own disc *Supa Sista*, which included the track "What???" which challenged mainstream rappers to a battle. But Rucker sets up the rules for the battle stating "no krissy, no thongs, no baby-boos or baby-daddies" and "no platinum or ice . . .," essentially challenging her male colleagues to rely simply on their wit and creativity, instead of the standard tropes of ghetto authenticity. In a more celebrated example, performance artist Sarah Jones stepped to the mike to hold mainstream hip-hop accountable with her track "Your Revolution" (on DJ Vadim's *USSR: Life from the Other Side*). "Your Revolution" is a riff from Gil Scott-Heron's "The Revolution Will Not Be Televised," arguably hip-hop's ur-text. On the track Jones takes shots at the sexist lyrics of artists like Biggie ("Big Poppa"), LL ("Doin' It"), and Shaggy ("Boombastic"). But in an ironic twist that perfectly captures the struggles of those who try to hold hip-hop accountable, Jones's lyrics were cited as "vulgar" by the FCC. A complaint was filed after the song was played on Portland, Oregon's WBOO in 1999.[50]

The protest efforts by the young black women at Spelman highlight a changing dynamic among critics of hip-hop's gender politics. According to Beverly Guy-Sheftall, director of the Women's Studies Program at Spelman College, "What made [the protest] interesting was that it was young people who are considered part of the hip-hop generation. . . . When older African-Americans make these complaints, it's seen as a generational issue."[51] Indeed it was in Guy-Sheftall's feminist theory class that Jennings, Bailey, and others debated the merits of organizing a boycott. According to Bailey, Guy-Sheftall was "the voice of reason. . . . If we were upset about [Nelly's] portrayal of African-American women in the video, our actions had to be equally powerful."[52] Guy-Sheftall adds that "Rarely do you have such an obvious case of theory and practice coming together in class."[53] Spelman College, notably, is the only historically black college in the country that has a full-fledged women's studies program. The fact that the "Tip-Drill" protest was cultivated within a distinct feminist and pro-feminist context speaks powerfully, again, to the importance of feminist thought within black communities. It also highlights the responsibility that I have, as a heterosexual black man to add my voice to those struggles, even if it's to a hip-hop beat.

Afterword

Why write a book like *New Black Man*? What's to be gained by calling forth a generation of pro-feminist, anti-homophobic, nurturing black men? Scholars all have an intellectual project, a basic issue that they seek to address during the course of their careers. My goal has always been to address the concept of black community. Although many have interpreted the fissures and crevices within the so-called black community (particularly in the post–civil-rights era) as evidence of weakness, I believe that a diversity of ideas and identities actually strengthens our communities. I've been committed to doing work that highlights the value of those who have been marginalized in our communities, including but not limited to black youth, black women (and black feminists in particular), and black gays and lesbians.

I've been equally committed to using my work and my civic voice to challenge the real violence—physical, rhetorical, and emotional—that we inflict on those marginalized bodies in our communities. It's not enough to close ranks around those who we marginalize; we need to take aim at the very forms of privilege that allow folks to continue to be marginalized. As a heterosexual black man in my late thirties, I have access to modes of privilege

within black communities and the larger society, namely patriarchy and social status. These are privileges that many of those
marginalized within our communities simply don't possess. *New
Black Man* is my attempt to talk openly and honestly about
those privileges, especially black male privilege, and to think
out loud about the ways that black men can develop relationships with their mothers, daughters, sisters, friends, and colleagues that are pro-feminist and anti-sexist. There's no doubt
in my mind that Black America must address sexism, misogyny,
and homophobia at this point in our history. Below are just
a few things for us to think about when pursuing the life of a
New Black Man.

Understanding Black Male Privilege

Too often when I discuss black male privilege with black men,
they fall back on defense mechanisms that highlight the effects
of racism and unemployment in the lives of black men. There's
no question that these issues are real challenges to black men,
but just because black men are under siege in White America,
it doesn't mean that they don't exhibit behaviors that do real
damage to others, particularly within black communities. What
many of these young men want to do is excuse the behavior of
black men because of the extenuating circumstances under
which black manhood is lived in our society. What they are
suggesting is that black male behaviors that oppress women,
children, and gays and lesbians in our community are under-
standable given the amount of oppression that some black men
face from White America. This is unacceptable because one
form of oppression cannot be used to justify another. Further-
more, it neglects the fact that others, some black women, for
example, are also oppressed by White America because of their
race and gender.

Countless conferences, books, pamphlets, articles, and online
discussions are devoted to the crises that black men face, and

the violence that is manifested against them, but there is comparatively little discussion of the very violence that black men often wield against black women. In fact, conversations about black male violence against black women and children are often interpreted as being part of the very racism that black men face. Those who speak out about black male violence are seen as traitors. We must get to a point where black male violence against black women, children, gays, and lesbians is openly challenged for what it is—behavior that is deeply harmful to the entire black community—and not just in the cases where the culprit is some young black male of the hip-hop generation. It has been too easy to blame the indiscretions and crimes of hip-hop generation figures like R. Kelly, Mystikal, or Tupac on the moral failings of the hip-hop generation, when we should be owning up to the fact that their behavior might have been influenced by their perceptions of how black male privilege operates in our communities.

Black Feminism is not the Enemy

One of the main attributes of black male privilege is the unwillingness or incapability to fully understand the plight of black women in our communities. Yes, there are acknowledgments of incidents where black woman are affected by blatant racism, but fewer when black women are affected because they are *black women* as opposed to being simply black people. Black feminism has sought to address this issue, creating a body of writings and activist events that highlight the conditions of black women globally. For example, it was not surprising that during the vice-presidential debate in October 2004 neither Vice-President Dick Cheney nor Democratic nominee John Edwards were aware that for black women between the ages of twenty-five and thirty-four, HIV disease was the largest cause of death. Tellingly, the debate was hosted by television journalist Gwen Ifill, an African-American woman. Black feminism has

sought to make such information available and a topic of conversation, especially among the black political leadership.

Much of the violence against black women happens close to
home, so it shouldn't be surprising that black men come under
close scrutiny and criticism by black feminism. Yes, some of
the criticism is very angry, and admittedly not all of it is con-
structive (as with criticisms of white racism), but it is absolutely
necessary in a society where black women's critical voices are
so often silenced. For those black men who don't understand
the anger that many black women feel toward them, it might
be helpful to think about the amount of anger that many blacks
still harbor toward whites, given the history of racism in this
country. Indeed, some black men have oppressed black women
in ways that closely resemble the historical oppression of blacks
by whites in American society.

Very often those black men who are critical of feminism
simply have not done their homework. They are responding
to hearsay they've heard on call-in talk shows or read online,
rather than actually reading any black feminist writings themselves. These men should check themselves, and check out
a book by Audre Lorde, June Jordan, Barbara Christian, Pat
Parker, Cheryl Clarke, Barbara Smith, Patricia Hill-Collins,
Jewelle Gomez, Beverly Guy-Sheftall, Johnetta Cole, Cathy
Cohen, Sharon Patricia Holland, Gwendolyn Pough, Joy James,
and Alice Walker, Sonia Sanchez, Nikki Giovanni, and Masani
Alexis DeVeaux—just a few of the women who have contributed
to the body of literature known as Black Feminist Thought.
Black feminism is wide ranging, and is concerned not only with
dealing with violence against black women and girls, but also
pressing issues of patriarchy, black women's healthcare, sex,
and sexuality, black women's education, and racism. We do no
justice to the legitimate issues that these women and others
have raised if we don't seriously engage their work.

Black men also need to be serious about finding out the
issues that affect the black women in their lives. For example,

some studies have shown that eighty percent of black women in the United States will suffer from some form of fibroid disease and yet most black men are unaware of the fact, largely because they view it, like menstrual cycles, as simply a "woman's issue." Could we ever imagine a malady that affected eighty percent of all black men in the United States that the majority of black women would be unaware of? Of course not.

Real Black Men are not Homophobes

The prevailing notion on the ground is that real black men ain't "fags." This concept not only goes against any notion of community, it also simply isn't true. Black gay men have been valuable contributors to all aspects of black life in the United States. The same faulty logic that suggests real black men ain't "fags" also suggests that black women are lesbians because black men have failed to live up to some "Strong Black Man" ideal, as if black lesbians were solely motivated by their displeasure with black men as opposed to their own social, cultural, and sexual desires. In either case, the presence of black gays and lesbians is often interpreted as a sign of failed black masculinity.

It's time that we start championing a movement where "real black men are not homophobes," given the damage that homophobia does in our community. Such a movement would encourage black men to forcefully challenge homophobia wherever they encounter it, whether it's expressed as heterosexist jokes on the *Tom Joyner in the Morning Show*, BET's *Comic View*, or in the kinds of homophobic violence, rhetorical and literal, that circulate regularly in our churches, on college campuses, in barbershops, within hip-hop, and other institutions within black communities. It's not enough for us to simply eradicate homophobia in our own lives, we need to make the message loud and clear that homophobia is not welcome in our communities. We also need to think differently about black masculinity and understand that black men exhibit a range of attitudes and behaviors that don't always fit neatly into some mythical notion of a "Strong Black Man." We do incredible damage to ourselves and to those around us by submitting to an idea that there is some little box that all black men must fit into. We are bigger than that.

Real Black Fathers are Loving Fathers

It has long been believed that the only responsibilities black men have in relation to their families are to provide financially and to dispense discipline. Although these are important aspects of parenting, this model of fatherhood does not allow black men to be emotionally available to their children and wives as nurturers. The idea that black men can be nurturers is often viewed skeptically, as evidence of some kind of weakness. Therefore, many black men who are unable to find work often think that they aren't good fathers because the only model of fatherhood they know is one where black men are, above all else, providers. I suspect this thinking can be directly correlated to the number of black men who have chosen to be involved in the illicit underground drug economy.

This narrow view of fatherhood can take men away from their sons and daughters by means of incarceration or worse, death, and it can prompt men to leave their families because they feel unfit as fathers if they fall upon hard times. We need black men to be there for their children, not just financially, but physically and emotionally. So it is crucial that we establish new rules of fatherhood that allow black men to be good fathers regardless of their temporary economic status.

Rethinking black fatherhood goes hand-in-hand with rethinking black masculinity. We need to applaud black fathers who see themselves as partners in the full range of parenting activities, and who take seriously their roles as nurturers. We need to build a model of black feminist fatherhood, one in which black men aren't just the protectors of their daughters, but also seriously consider how black girls and black women live in the world and the challenges and dangers that they are liable to face. In a world where young black girls are so often silenced and invisible, black fathers have a responsibility, along with black mothers, to create the spaces where the plight of black girls is taken seriously. This also requires sensitizing young black boys, both our sons and those that we come in contact with on a regular basis, to the importance of black girls and black women.

Hip-Hop is not the Enemy, but it is a Problem

Like it or not, hip-hop is the soundtrack of black youth. It's been so easy to point to the moral failings of the hip-hop generation, particularly in relation to the sexism, misogyny, and homophobia that circulates in some of the music and videos, but those moral failings are often just a reflection of how the larger society and black communities think about black women, children, gays, and lesbians. Many criticisms of hip-hop simply deflect attention from equally disturbing practices within more traditional and acceptable black institutions. Too often, the criticisms of hip-hop are done without a real understanding of how ideas, knowledge, language, emotions, and relationships are cultivated by the hip-hop generation. It's not as if the hip-hop generation is beyond scrutiny, but if our elders are going to hold us accountable, they should at least make an effort to understand our worldview and the reasons why we make the choices we make. The world that the post–civil-rights generation(s) inhabits is fundamentally different from the one that produced the freedom movement of the 1950s and 1960s, and our elders need to acknowledge that fact. Our demons are not their demons, and our elders do us no good pretending that our current dilemma is somehow the product of our moral failings and our inability to pay homage to the freedom fighters who came before us. That said, the hip-hop generation also needs to appreciate the sacrifices made by our elders and accept that there are worthwhile lessons to be learned from their examples.

Just as hip-hop has been used to help politicize the hip-hop generation, it must also be used to create better gender relationships within the hip-hop generation. We need to make language available to young men in hip-hop that will help them rethink their gender politics. Young men often see hip-hop as a haven to articulate their frustrations with women—girlfriends, mothers, baby-mamas, groupies—but they are rarely capable of turning the critique upon themselves in order to interrogate their own roles in creating and maintaining dysfunctional relationships with women. The dialogue with young men is beginning in the work of black feminists of the hip-hop generation—Gwendolyn Pough and Joan Morgan come immediately to mind—and it is valuable work that I hope will continue to engage hip-hop music and those who listen and produce it, so that an honest conversation takes place, not just scolding and finger-wagging.

Young black women, of course, are also learning about and expressing their gender and sexuality through hip-hop. Talk about women and hip-hop, or hip-hop and gender, is often reduced to issues of misogyny and homophobia. Although these critiques *must* be made, the conversation typically remains focused on how men portray women in their lyrics and music videos. Rarely do we discuss how women use hip-hop to articulate their view of the world, a view that may or may not be predicated on what the men in hip-hop (or their lives) might be doing. For example, many black women hip-hop artists, scholars, and journalists speak about "desire" (sexual and otherwise) and the ways that women artists articulate desire in their art. Unfortunately, these issues are rarely discussed in mainstream discussions about hip-hop. Perhaps some of the critical energy focused so much on what black men in hip-hop are saying about women would be better spent by learning to listen to the voices of black women themselves.

Becoming a New Black Man

> I am a man of my times, but the times don't know it yet!
>
> Erik Todd Dellums as Bayard Rustin in *Boycott*

Finally, it is important the readers remember that I am not *the* New Black Man, but rather that the New Black Man is a metaphor for an imagined life—a way to be "strong" as a black man in new ways: strong commitment to diversity in our communities, strong support for women and feminism, and strong faith in love and the value of listening. I struggle, and often falter, to live up to these ideals every day of my life. It's a challenge, but one I know is well worth facing for myself, for my wife, and for my beautiful daughters. After reading these words, I hope you will join me, men and women, in making the New Black Man the man of our times.

Endnotes

Chapter 1

1. Bob Herbert, "Who Will Help the Black Man?" *New York Times* (December 4, 1994), 72.
2. Ibid., 74.
3. Henry L. Davis and Jerry Zremski, "Use of Drugs, Rough Sex Eyed for Role in Outbreak," *The Buffalo News*, (November 2, 1997), 1A.
4. See Thomas Shevory's thoughtful study, *The Notorious H.I.V.* (Minneapolis, University of Minnesota Press, 2004).
5. Jennifer Frey, "Nushawn's Girls," *Washington Post* (June 1, 1999), C01.
6. Donn Esmonde, "Williams Described as a Charmer," *Buffalo News* (October 30, 1997), 1A.
7. Jennifer Tanaka and Gregory Beals, "The Victims' Stories: He Charmed the Lost and the Unwanted," *Newsweek* (November 10, 1997), 55.
8. Ibid., 56.
9. Agnes Palazzetti, "Suspect Kept Score," *The Buffalo News* (October 29, 1997), 1A.
10. Lisa Kennedy, "The Miseducation of Nushawn Williams" at www.poz.com/archive/august2000/inside/nushawnwilliams.html (August 2000).
11. Saundra Smokes, "White Victims Made AIDS Predator Big News," *USA Today* (November 7, 1997), 25.
12. Thomas Shevory, "Constructing Nushawn: AIDS, Race, and Media Politics" (unpublished paper), Meeting of the American Political Science Association (September 2, 1998).
13. "Is There No Shame" (editorial), *New York Daily News* (November 1, 1997), 16.
14. Anthony Cardinale, "HIV Predator Stayed in Touch with Some Victims," *Buffalo News* (August 10, 2001), B20.
15. "Is There No Shame," 16.
16. See Associated Press, "Morgan Awarded $796,000," *Chicago Sun-Times* (November 17, 1993), 6; Shannon Tangonan, "Railroad Apologizes to Passenger Frisked Because of His Race," *USA Today* (May 10, 1995), 2A; Peter May and

161

Jerry Thomas, "Officers Hold Celtic at Gun Point," *Boston Globe* (September 22, 1990), 1.

17. Bryonn Bain, "Walking While Black: The Bill of Rights for Black Men," *The Village Voice* (April 26, 2000).

18. Daniel Jeffreys, "'They're Poisoning Our Kids': Is Gangsta Rap All a White Conspiracy," *The Independent* (July 31, 1995), 2.

19. Ibid., 3.

20. Allison Samuels "Battle for the Soul of Hip-Hop: Is Rap Increasingly Driven by Sex, Violence, and Money Going Too Far?" *Newsweek* (October 9, 2000), 58.

21. M. Rick Turner, "What's Happening to Our 'Talented Tenth'," *Black Issues in Higher Education* (December 7, 2000), 152.

22. See W.E.B. DuBois, The Souls of Black Folk, (Chicago: A.C. McClurg and Co., 1903).

23. Turner, 152.

24. Ibid., 152.

25. Ibid., 152.

26. Larry Olmstead, "From Powerful Pulpit, a Moral Warrior Takes Aim," *New York Times* (June 5, 1993), 23.

27. See Mark Anthony Neal, *What the Music Said: Black Popular Music and Black Public Culture* (New York: Routledge, 1999).

28. Michael Marriot, "Harlem Pastor to Campaign Against Rap Lyrics," *New York Times* (May 8, 1993), 24.

29. Olmstead, 23.

30. To be fair, Butts was the only Harlem minister who supported African Americans Against Violence (AAAs), a group formed in the aftermath of a planned homecoming celebration for convicted rapist, boxer Mike Tyson.

31. Frances E. Wood, "'Take My Yoke Upon You': The Role of the Church in the Oppression of African-American Women," in *A Troubling in My Soul: Womanist Perspectives on Evil and Suffering*, ed. Emilie M. Townes (Maryknoll, NY: Orbis, 1993), 39.

32. Laura Sessions Stepp, "Blacks Vs. Feminist: A Very American War in a Very American Church," *Washington Post* (October 20, 1985), C1.

33. Ibid., C1.

34. Candice M. Jenkins, "Queering Black Patriarchy: The Salvific Wish and Masculine Possibility in Alice Walker's *The Color Purple*," *Modern Fiction Studies* 48.4 (2002), 973.

35. Marcia L. Dyson, "When Preachers Prey," *Essence Magazine* (May 1998), 120.

36. Ibid., 122.

37. Ibid., 122.

38. Anthony King, "'Barbershop' Controversy: Black Heroes Ought to Be Free of Barbs," *Atlanta Journal and Constitution* (October 10, 2002), 19A.

39. Ibid., 19A.

40. Scott Bowles, "'Barbershop' Dialogue Too Cutting, Some Say," *USA Today* (September 19, 2002), 1D.

41. Ibid., 1D.

42. William Jelani Cobb, "Forty Years, Are We Free at Last?" at www.africana.com/articles/daily/ht20030828march.asp, (August 28, 2003).

43. Mary Mitchell, "Critics of 'Barbershop' Distorting Its Message," *Chicago Sun-Times* (September 29, 2002), 16.

44. Ibid., 16.
45. Larry Copeland, "Jesse Jackson Reveals Affair," USA Today (January 19, 2001), 3A.
46. Michael Eric Dyson, I May Not Get There With You: The True Martin Luther King (New York: Free Press, 2000), 160.
47. Thelma Golden, "My Brother," in Black Male: Representations of Masculinity in Contemporary American Art (New York: Whitney Museum of American Art, 1994), 19.
48. Clyde Taylor, "The Game," in Black Male: Representations of Masculinity in Contemporary American Art (New York: Whitney Museum of American Art, 1994), 169.
49. See Du Bois, The Souls of Black Folk and Alain Locke, The New Negro (New York: A. and C. Boni, 1925).
50. Kevin K. Gaines, Uplifting the Race: Black Leadership, Politics, and Culture in the Twentieth Century (Chapel Hill, NC: The University of North Carolina Press), 69.
51. Joseph H. Brown, "'Ghettopoly' No Bigger Insult Than MTV Rap," Tampa Tribune (October 19, 2003), 6.
52. Gaines, 169.
53. News release, "Minister Louis Farrakhan Calls for One Million Man March," The Final Call (December 14, 1994).
54. Louis Farrakhan, "A Holy Day of Atonement and Reconciliation: October 16, 1995," The Final Call (September, 1995).
55. Louis Farrakhan, "Million Man March Pledge," at www.finalcall.com/national.anniversary/mmm-pledge.html.
56. Debra Dickerson, "Queen for a Day?" The New Republic (November 6, 1995), 22.
57. News release, "Minister Louis Farrakhan Calls for One Million Man March," The Final Call (December 14, 1994).
58. Dickerson, 22.
59. Houston A. Baker, Jr., Critical Memory: Public Spheres, African-American Writing, and Black Fathers and Sons in America (Athens, GA: The University of Georgia Press, 2001), 60.
60. Men Stopping Violence "Dear Minister Farrakhan: A Letter," in Traps: African American Men on Gender and Sexuality, ed. Rudolph P. Byrd and Beverly Guy-Sheftall (Bloomington, IN: Indiana University Press, 2001), 268.
61. Louis Farrakhan, "Farrakhan on Race, Politics, and the News Media," New York Times (April 17, 1984), 16.
62. Robert Reid-Pharr, Black Gay Man: Essays (New York: New York University Press, 2001), 165–166.
63. Debby Lynn Davis, "Black Gay Men Seek Spot in Million Event," Milwaukee Journal Sentinel (October 9, 1995), 3.
64. Ibid., 3.
65. Michael A. Fletcher, "Supporting March a Big Step for Some," Washington Post (October 11, 1995), A01.
66. David W. Dunlap, "Gay Blacks in Quandary Over Farrakhan's March," New York Times (October 8, 1995), 24.
67. Salim Muwakkil, "Divided Loyalties," In These Times (February 17, 1997), 24.
68. Ibid., 24.
69. Jenkins, 973.

70. See Mark Anthony Neal's "Baby Mama (Drama) and Baby Daddy (Trauma): Post-Soul Gender Relations," in *Soul Babies: Black Popular Culture and the Post-Soul Aesthetic* (New York: Routledge, 2002).
71. News release, "Minister Louis Farrakhan Calls for One Million Man March," *The Final Call* (December 14, 1994).
72. Maurice O. Wallace, *Constructing the Black Masculine: Identity and Ideality in African American Men's Literature and Culture, 1775-1995* (Durham, NC: Duke University Press, 2002), 54.
73. Ibid., 54.
74. Ibid., 75.
75. Norm R. Allen, Jr., "Reactionary Black Nationalism: Authoritarianism in the Name of Freedom," *Free Inquiry* (Fall 1995), 10.
76. Richard Gilman, quoted on the cover of *Soul On Ice*.
77. Eldridge Cleaver, *Soul On Ice* (New York: Dell, 1968), 14.
78. Ibid., 103.
79. Daniel Patrick Moynihan, "The Negro Family: The Case for National Action," in *The Moynihan Report and the Politics of Controversy*, ed. Lee Rainwater and William L. Yancey (Cambridge, MA: MIT Press, 1967) 43.
80. Ibid., 75.
81. Ibid., 75.
82. Jill Nelson, *Straight, No Chaser: How I Became a Grown-Up Black Woman* (New York: Putnam, 1997), 161.
83. Robert Reid-Pharr, *Black Gay Man: Essays* (New York: New York University Press, 2001), 158.
84. Ibid., 161.

Chapter 2

1. Unpublished journal, quoted in Alexis DeVeaux's *Warrior Poet: A Biography of Audre Lorde* (New York: Norton), 203.
2. Jacqueline Trescott, "Passions Over 'Purple'; Anger and Unease Over Film's Depiction of Black Men," *Washington Post* (February 5, 1986), C1.
3. Ibid., C1.
4. Sandra Hollin Flowers, "*Colored Girls*: Textbook for the Eighties," *Black American Literature Forum*, Vol. 15, No. 2 (Summer, 1981), 54.
5. Ntozake Shange, *for colored girls who have considered suicide/when the rainbow is enuf* (New York: Macmillan, 1977), 43.
6. Neal A. Lester, "Shange's Men: *For Colored Girls Revisited*, and Movement Beyond," *African-American Review*, Vol. 26, No. 2 (Summer 1992), 319.
7. Michele Wallace, *Black Macho and the Myth of the Superwomen* (New York: Dial, 1979), 23.
8. Ibid., 34.
9. Stanley Crouch, "Aunt Jemima Don't Like Uncle Ben," in *Notes of a Hanging Judge: Essays and Reviews, 1979–1989* (New York: Oxford University Press, 1990), 29.
10. Mel Watkins, "Sexism, Racism and Black Women Writers," *New York Times* (June 15, 1986), Section 7, page 1.
11. Calvin Hernton, "The Sexual Mountain and Black Women Writers," *Black American Literature Forum*, Vol. 18, No. 4 (Winter, 1984), 140.
12. Jewelle Gomez, *Forty-Three Septembers* (Ithaca, NY: Firebrand, 1993), 121.

13. Ibid., 121.
14. Jewelle Gomez, "Finding Our Voice," *Essence Magazine* (May 1995), 198.
15. Karen Boorstein, "Beyond Black Macho: An Interview with Michele Wallace," *Black American Literature Forum*, Vol. 18, No. 4 (Winter, 1984), 164.
16. Wallace, xxxviii.
17. Boorstein, 165.
18. Nathan and Julia Hare, *The Endangered Black Family: Coping with the Unisexualization and Coming Extinction of the Black Race* (San Francisco: Black Think Tank, 1984), 139.
19. Derrick Z. Jackson, "Hardly a Lynch Victim," *The Boston Globe* (October 16, 1991), 15.
20. Devon Carbado, "Black Male Racial Victimhood," *Callaloo* 21.2 (1998), 344–345.
21. Barbara Smith, "Toward a Black Feminist Criticism," *Conditions: Two 1* (1977), 25–44; Deborah E. McDowell, "New Directions for Black Feminist Criticism," *Black American Literature Forum 14* (1980), 153–159; Barbara Christian, "The Race for Theory," *Cultural Critique 6* (Spring 1987), 51–63.
22. bell hooks, *Yearning: Race, Gender and Cultural Politics*, (Boston: South End Press, 1990), 74.
23. Ibid., 75.
24. Mark Anthony Neal, "And God Created Woman," *The Leader* (March 29, 1993), 11.
25. Audre Lorde, *Sister Outsider* (Freedom, CA: Crossing Press, 1984), 54.
26. Ibid., 54.
27. Ibid., 56.
28. Ibid., 56–57.
29. See Stanlie M. James and Abena Busia, eds. *Theorizing Black Feminisms* (New York: Routledge, 1993).
30. Patricia Hill-Collins, *Black Feminist Thought: Knowledge, Consciousness and the Politics of Empowerment* (New York: Routledge, 1990), 15.
31. See Neal *What the Music Said: Black Popular Culture and Black Public Culture* (New York: Routledge, 1999); *Soul Babies: Black Popular Culture and the Post-Soul Aesthetic* (New York: Routledge, 2002); "The Tortured Soul of Marvin Gaye and R. Kelly," Da Capo Best Music Writing 2004 (New York: Da Capo Press, 2004).
32. Hill-Collins, 69.
33. Ibid., 85.
34. Gomez, *Forty-Three Septembers*, 48.
35. Ibid., 48.
36. Ibid., 51.
37. Ibid., 59.
38. Ibid., 58.
39. Ibid., 54.
40. Ibid., 54.
41. Barbara Ransby, "Fear of a Black Feminist Planet," *In These Times* (July 12, 1998), 20.
42. Gary L. Lemons, "'When and Where [We] Enter': In Search of a Feminist Forefather—Reclaiming the *Womanist* Legacy of W.E.B. Du Bois," in *Traps: African-American Men on Gender and Sexuality*, ed. Rudolph P. Byrd and Beverley Guy-Sheftall (Bloomington, IN: Indiana University Press, 2001), 83.

43. Greg Tate, *Flyboy in the Buttermilk: Essays on Contemporary America* (New York: Simon & Schuster, 1992), 86.
44. Miles Davis with Quincy Troupe, *Miles: The Autobiography* (New York: Simon & Schuster, 1989), 366.
45. Pearl Cleage, *Mad at Miles: A Blackwoman's Guide to Truth* (Southfield, MI: Cleage Group, 1990), 13.
46. Hazel V. Carby makes the convincing argument that Davis's genius was inextricably tied to his abuses of women. Carby writes, "I think it is very important to challenge the apparent distance between Davis's violence against women and the 'genius' of his music, as if they were enacted on different planes. . . . The various women described in *Miles* are carefully given their place in his material world: they may service his bodily sexual and physical needs, but are albatrosses around his neck when he wants to fly with other men in the musical realm of 'genius' and performance." (*Race Men*, Cambridge, MA: Harvard University Press, 1998, 144).
47. Ibid., 15.
48. "Violence Is Reflected in Actions as Well as Words," *USA Today* (June 21, 1991), 4D.
49. Chris Morris, "TV Host Barnes Pumps Out $23 Mil Suit Against NWA," *Billboard* (July 13, 1991), 9.
50. Morris, "N.W.A. Member Dr. Dre Pleads No Contest On Attack Charge," *Billboard* (September 7, 1991), 11.
51. Tricia Rose, *Black Noise: Rap Music and Black Culture in Contemporary America*, (Hanover, CT: Wesleyan University Press, 1994), 179.
52. Ibid., 179.
53. Pearl Cleage, *Deals with the Devil and Other Reasons to Riot* (New York: Ballantine, 1994), 154.
54. Quoted in Lena Williams, "Black Woman's Book Starts a Predictable Storm," *New York Times* (October 2, 1990), 11.
55. Quoted in Dorothy Gilliam, "Sick, Distorted Thinking," *Washington Post* (October 11, 1990), D3.
56. Quoted in Rose, 179.
57. Tate, 125.
58. Ibid., 252.
59. For examples of critiques of Lee's cinematic gender politics see Michele Wallace, "Spike Lee and Black Women," *The Nation* (June 1988), 800–803; "Doing the Right Thing," *Art Forum International* (October 1989), 20–22; Valerie Smith, *Not Just Race, Not Just Gender: Black Feminist Readings* (New York: Routledge, 1998), 89–119; Wahneema Lubiano, "But Compared to What?: Reading Realism, Representation, and Essentialism in *School Daze, Do the Right Thing*, and the Spike Lee Discourse," *Black American Literature Forum* Vol. 25, No. 2 (Summer 1991), 253–282.
60. Tate, 285.
61. Michael Awkward, Negotiating Difference: Race, Gender, and the Politics of Positionality (Chicago: University of Chicago Press, 49.
62. Ibid., 51.
63. Michael Awkward, *Scenes of Instruction: A Memoir* (Durham, NC: Duke University Press, 1999), 4.
64. Ibid., 5.

65. Michele Wallace, *Invisibility Blues: From Pop to Theory* (London: Verso, 1990), 251.
66. Joy James, *Shadowboxing: Representations of Black Feminist Politics* (New York: St. Martin's, 1999), 157.
67. David D. Kirkpatrick, "On Long-Lost Pages, A Female Slave's Voice," *New York Times* (November 11, 2001), 1.
68. David Ikard, "Love Jones: A Black Male Feminist Critique of Chester Himes's *If He Hollers Let Him Go*," *African American Review* Vol. 36, No. 2 (2002), 310.
69. Kevin Powell, "The Sexist in Me," in *Traps*, ed. Byrd and Guy-Sheftall, 221.
70. Powell, *Keepin' It Real: Post-MTV Reflections on Race, Sex and Politics* (New York: Ballantine, 1997), 132.
71. Ibid., 153.
72. Powell, *Who's Gonna Take the Weight? Manhood, Race, and Power in America* (New York: Three Rivers, 2003), 65.
73. Ibid.
74. Ibid., 49.

Chapter 3

1. Essex Hemphill, "In an Afternoon Light," in *Brother to Brother*, ed. Essex Hemphill (Boston: Allyson, 1991), 258.
2. Boogie Down Productions, "Ya Strugglin'" from *Edutainment*.
3. Fannie Lou Hamer and Amzie and Ruth Moore were part of the class of organic activists who openly challenged racial segregation and white supremacy in Mississippi. See Charles Payne's *I've Got the Light of Freedom: The Organizing Tradition and the Mississippi Freedom Struggle* (Berkeley: University of California Press, 1996).
4. Ronald Simmons, "Some Thoughts on the Challenge Facing Black Gay Intellectuals," in *Brother to Brother*, ed. Essex Hemphill (Boston: Allyson, 1991), 211.
5. Daniel Jenkins, "Winans Song's Anti-gay Message Does Harm," *Billboard* (December 13, 1997), 8–10; Alan Frutkin, "The Gospel Truth," *The Advocate* (November 25, 1997), 22.
6. Rhonda M. Williams, "Living at the Crossroads: Explorations in Race, Nationality, Sexuality, and Gender," in *The House that Race Built: Black Americans, U.S. Terrain*, ed. Wahneema Lubiano (New York: Pantheon, 1997), 139.
7. E. Patrick Johnson, "Strange Fruit: A Performance about Identity Politics," *The Drama Review* Vol. 47, No. 2 (Summer 2003), 91.
8. Phillip Brain Harper, *Are We Not Men?: Masculine Identity and the Problem of African-American Identity* (New York: Oxford University Press, 1996), 11.
9. Williams, 141.
10. Cathy J. Cohen, *The Boundaries of Blackness: AIDs and the Breakdown of Black Politics* (Chicago: University of Chicago Press, 1999), 35.
11. Sharon Patricia Holland, *Raising the Dead: Readings of Death and (Black) Subjectivity* (Durham, NC: Duke University Press, 2000), 120.
12. See Jervis Anderson, *Bayard Rustin: Troubles I've Seen* (New York: HarperCollins, 1997); John D'Emilio, *Lost Prophet: The Life and Times of Bayard Rustin* (New York: Free Press, 2003).
13. Simmons, 211.

14. Quoted in Laura Putre, "Amazing Grace and Resolve," *The Advocate* (February 19, 2002), 23.
15. The Paradise Garage was one of the most well-known dance clubs in New York City during the 1980s that catered to a largely homosexual clientele.
16. Craig Seymour, "Gays Feel Left Out of Morehouse Brotherhood," *Atlanta Journal-Constitution* (December 29, 2002), 1A.
17. Quoted in Steve Sternberg, "The Danger of Living 'Down Low'," *USA Today* (March 15, 2001), 1D.
18. Benoit Denizet-Lewis, "Double Lives on the Down Low," *New York Times* (August 3, 2003), Section 6, 28.
19. Fact Sheet—HIV/AIDS Among African Americans at www.cdc.gov/hiv/pubs/Facts/afam.htm.
20. To give an indication of how much times have changed, Linda Villarosa's report on increasing HIV rates among black women was a front page story in the *New York Times*. See Linda Villarosa, "AIDS Fears Grow for Black Women," *New York Times* (April 5, 2004), 1.
21. Denizet-Lewis, 28.
22. Quoted in Guy Trebay, "Homo Thugz Blow Up the Spot," *The Village Voice* (February 8, 2000).
23. Quoted in Trebay.
24. Quoted in Greg Herren, "I Don't Discuss My Have: Frank Words from James Earl Hardy about Racism, Homophobia, Hip-Hop and Shopping at Macy's," *Lambda Book Report* (September 2001), 9.
25. Isiaah Crawford, Kevin W. Allison, Brian D. Zamboni, and Tomas Soto, "The Influence of Dual-Identity Development on the Psychological Functioning of African-American Gay and Bisexual Men," *The Journal of Sex Research* Vol. 39, No. 3 (August 2002), 186.
26. Herron, 9.
27. Crawford et al., 186.
28. Quoted in Makebra Anderson, "Undercover Brothers: Life on the 'Down Low'," *Los Angeles Sentinel* (June 12, 2002), A1.
29. Quoted in Denizet-Lewis, 28.
30. Thomas Glave, "The Final Inning," in *Whose Song? And Other Short Stories* (San Francisco: City Lights, 2000), 172–173.
31. "HIV/AIDS Among African Americans" at www.cdc.gov/hiv/pubs/Facts/afam.pdf.
32. Linda Villarosa, "AIDS Fears Grow for Black Women," *New York Times* (April 5, 2004), 1A. See also Sharon Lerner, "Black Women and HIV," *The Village Voice* (July 25, 2000).
33. Karen Hawkins, "The Changing Face of AIDs," *In These Times* (August 11, 2003), 23.
34. Cohen, 201–202.
35. Quoted in Denise Hollinshed and Jennifer LaFleur, "The Changing Face of AIDS," *St. Louis Post-Dispatch* (April 21, 2002), A1.
36. Sternberg, 1D.
37. David Wahlberg, "HIV Study is Chilling to Black College Campuses," *Atlanta Journal-Constitution* (March 11, 2004), 1A.

38. Cynthia Tucker, "Blacks Flee Gays, Can't Flee AIDS," *Atlanta Journal-Constitution* (March 14, 2004), 8D.
39. E. Patrick Johnson, *Appropriating Blackness: Performance and the Politics of Authenticity* (Durham, NC: Duke University Press, 2003), 68.
40. Quoted in James Dowd, "Back to the Foundation—Bishop G.E. Patterson, Leader COGIC—Church Standing Firm as Culture Shifts," *The Commercial Appeal* (November 9, 2003), A1.
41. Quoted in Cindy Wolff, "Houses Divided," *The Commercial Appeal* (November 2, 2003), D1.
42. Ta-Nehisi Coates, "Queer Eye for the Black Guy," *The Village Voice* (September 24–30, 2003).
43. Quoted in Jim Tharpe, "Pastors Send 'Clear' Message," *Atlanta Journal Constitution* (March 1, 2004), 1B.
44. Quoted in Michael Paulson, "Black Clergy Rejection Stirs Gay Marriage Backers," *Boston Globe* (February 10, 2004), B1.
45. Jabari Asim, "Black Churches and Gay Marriage," *Washington Post* (November 24, 2003).
46. Kelly Brown Douglas, "Breaking the Chains," *The Other Side* (September & October 2000), 17–18.
47. Ibid., 18.
48. Ibid., 17, 19.
49. Ibid., 19.
50. Quoted in Lynette Clemetson, "Both Sides Court Black Churches in the Battle Over Gay Marriage," *New Times* (March 1, 2004), 1A.
51. Paulson, B1.
52. Reverend Osagyefo Uhuru Sekou, *UrbanSouls* (St. Louis, MO: Urban Press, 2001), 51.
53. Quoted in Asim.
54. Coates. Village Voice (September 24-30, 2003).
55. Alexis DeVeaux, *Warrior Poet: A Biography of Audre Lorde* (New York: Norton, 2004), 324–325.
56. De Veaux, 327.
57. Clemetson, A1.
58. Kelly Cogswell and Ana Simo, "Erasing Sakia: Who's to Blame?" *The Gully* (June 3, 2003).
59. Alicia Banks, "A Eulogy for Sakia Gunn, An Eternal Sista Warrior" at www.geocities.com/ambwww/sakia.htm.
60. Devon Carbado, "Black Male Racial Victimhood," *Callaloo* 21.2 (1998), 344–345.
61. "Officers Accused of Beating Woman," *New York Daily News* (March 2, 2000).
62. Cogswell and Sino, "Erasing Sakia: Who's to Blame?"
63. Pat Reavy and Brian Kates, "Utah Girl Snatched from Bed," *New York Daily News* (June 6, 2002), 10.
64. "Police Search for Sign of Girl," *Milwaukee Journal Sentinel* (May 5, 2002), 2B.
65. James H. Burnett III, "Alexis' Story to Get National Exposure During CNN Show Tonight," *Milwaukee Journal Sentinel* (June 19, 2002), 3B.
66. Kim Pearson, "No Justice, No Peace and No More Press for Gunn, Baraka and Holmes" *Professor Kim's News Notes* (February 25, 2004).

Chapter 4

1. Thaddeus Goodavage, "Are You My Father?" in *Father Songs: Testimonies by African-American Sons and Daughters*, ed. Gloria Wade-Gayles (Boston: Beacon, 1997), 23.
2. Nancy E. Dowd, *Redefining Fatherhood* (New York: New York University Press, 2000), 73.
3. Quoted in "They Call Them Mr. Mom; A Growing Number of Black Fathers Raise Daughters and Sons by Themselves," *Ebony* (June 1991), 52.
4. Scott Coltrane, "Father-Child Relationships and the Status of Women: A Cross-Cultural Study," *The American Journal of Sociology*, Vol. 93, No. 5 (March, 1988), 1089.
5. Scott Coltrane and Masako Ishii-Kuntz, "Men's Housework: A Life Course Perspective," *Journal of Marriage and the Family*, Vol. 54, No. 1 (February, 1992), 54.
6. See the American Sleep Apnea Association website (www.sleepapnea.org).
7. Ross D. Parke and Armin A. Brott, *Throwaway Dads: The Myths and Barriers that Keep Men from Being the Fathers They Want to Be* (New York: Houghton Mifflin, 1999), 77.
8. Parke and Brott, 78.
9. Quoted in Kyle D. Pruett, *The Nurturing Father* (New York: Warner, 1987), 59.
10. Isaac D. Balbus, *Emotional Rescue: The Theory and Practice of a Feminist Father* (New York: Routledge, 1998), 104.
11. Parke and Brott, 101.
12. George Vecsey, "More Bench for Darren This Time," *New York Times* (October 26, 2002), D1.
13. Tom Stanton, *Hank Aaron and the Home Run that Changed America* (New York: Morrow), 141.
14. Hal Bodley, "Baker is the Man Among Giants," *USA Today* (October 29, 2002), 4C.
15. Goodavage, 22.
16. Jonetta Rose Barras, *Whatever Happened to Daddy's Little Girl?: The Impact of Fatherlessness on Black Women* (New York: Ballantine, 2000), 39.
17. Dowd, 181.
18. Pruett, 281.
19. Louise B. Silverstein, "Fathering Is a Feminist Issue," *Psychology of Women Quarterly*, 20 (1996), 31.
20. Quoted in Rose Barras, 137.
21. Joan Morgan, *When Chickenheads Come Home to Roost: My Life s a Hip-Hop Feminist* (New York: Simon & Schuster, 1999), 126.
22. Rose Barras, 1.
23. Interview with the author, May 10, 2004.
24. Interview with the author, May 16, 2004.
25. Parke and Brott, 10.
26. Interview with author, May 14, 2004.
27. Interview with author, May 21, 2004.
28. Coltrane, 1089.
29. Aaron Freeman, "Notes of a Feminist Dad" at www.aaronfreeman.com/writer/femdad.html.
30. Parke and Brott, 10.
31. Silverstein, 30.

32. Silverstein, 4.
33. Mark Anthony Neal, *Soul Babies:Black Popular Culture and the Post-Soul Aesthetic* (New York: Routledge, 2002), 13.
34. Abdon M. Pallasch and Jim DeRogatis, "R&B Superstar Hit with 21 Counts of Child Porn," *Chicago Sun-Times* (June 6, 2002), 6.
35. Jim DeRogatis and Abdon M. Pallasch, "City Police Investigate R&B Singer R. Kelly in Sex Tape," *Chicago Sun-Times* (February 8, 2002), 1.
36. Jim DeRogatis and Abdon M. Pallasch, "R. Kelly Report Sparks Anger," *Chicago Sun-Times* (December 22, 2000), 3.
37. Mary Houlihan, "Kelly Tunes Get Boot at One Station," *Chicago Sun-Times* (June 6, 2002), 8.
38. Mary Mitchell, "Latest Allegation Unlikely to Get Kelly in Big Trouble," *Chicago Sun-Times* (February 14, 2002), 14.
39. Glenn Gaboa, "A War of Words," *Newsday* (December 21, 2003), 22.
40. Pearl Cleage, *Mad at Miles: A Blackwoman's Guide to Truth* (Southfield, MI: Cleage Group,1990), 20.

Chapter 5

1. Franki V. Ransom, "Black Women Launch Attack on 'Gangsta' Rap," *Times-Picayune* (December 23, 1993), A8.
2. Judith Weinraub, "Delores Tucker, Gangsta Buster," *Washington Post* (November 29, 1995), C01.
3. Richard Harrington, "The Rap on the Interscope Split," *Washington Post* (October 04, 1995), B07.
4. Marlene Cimons, "The Odd Couple of America's Debate on Values," *Chicago Sun-Times* (July 7, 1995).
5. Alexandra Marks, "Turning Up the Volume on 'Gangsta Rap' Debate," Christian *Science Monitor* (August 18, 1995), 1.
6. The ads depicted then-Democratic presidential candidate Governor Michael Dukakis of Massachusetts as "soft" on crime.
7. Stanley Crouch, "Hip-Hop's Thugs Hit New Low," *New York Daily News* (August 11, 2003), 35.
8. Adero Robinson, "Editorial: 'Pimps' an Embarrassment to Black Culture" *Columbus Dispatch* (May 6, 2004), 10A.
9. John Robinson, "Player's Club," *The Guardian* (September 20, 2003), 8.
10. Robin D.G. Kelley, "A Jazz Genius in the Guise of a Hustler," *New York Times* (May 13, 2001), AR1.
11. Quoted in Nekesa Mumbi Moody, "Pimps: The New 'Gangstas' of Rap," *Associated Press* (July 21, 2003).
12. David Segal, "Pimpin' Power; A Street Persona Finds Respect in the Hip-Hop and Pop Cultures," *Washington Post* (August 6, 2000), G01.
13. Jane O. Hansen, "World of Pimps is Sordid, Scary, But Is it Racketeering?" *Atlanta Journal-Constitution* (April 8, 2001), 1A.
14. Hansen, "Flashy Pimp Shindig Stirs Outrage in Atlanta," *Atlanta Journal-Constitution* (February 1, 2003), 1A.
15. Suzanne Simpson, "The Player's Ball," *Black Renaissance/Renaissance Noire* (Winter 1999), 94.
16. Quoted in Moody.

17. Beth Coleman, "Pimp Notes on Autonomy," in *Everything But the Burden: What White People Are Taking from Black Culture*, ed. Greg Tate (New York: Broadway Books, 2003), 80.
18. Eithne Quinn, "'Who's the Mack?': The Performativity and Politics of the Pimp Figure in Gangsta Rap," *Journal of American Studies*, 34 (2000), 123–124.
19. Ibid., 125.
20. Ibid., 125.
21. Quoted in Moody.
22. "Snoop Dogg: Where Are the Topless Black Girls?" *Associated Press* (June 24, 2003).
23. "The Latest Libations from the Nation's Beverage Makers," *Beverage Aisle* (October 2003).
24. Quoted in Sylvester Brown, "Nelly Has a Way with Words, Especially When it Comes to Selling Pimp Juice," *St. Louis Post-Dispatch* (September 14, 2003), C2.
25. Quoted in Clarence Page, "Why Nellys Pimp Juice Is Nothing But Poison," *New York Newsday* (September 16, 2003), A30.
26. Clarence Page, "Why Nellys Pimp Juice Is Nothing But Poison," *New York Newsday* (September 16, 2003), A30.
27. Michael Eric Dyson and Tavis Smiley, "Rebirth and Fascination with Pimp in Hip-Hop Culture," *National Public Radio* (October 2, 2003).
28. Brown, C2.
29. Natalie Hopkinson, "'Pimp' Show at Howard is by Definition Controversial," *Washington Post* (November 14, 2002), C01.
30. Elizabeth F. Farrell, "It's Gettin' Hot in Here," *Chronicle of Higher Education* (June 4, 2004), 27.
31. Gracie Bonds Staples and Vikki Conwell, "Spelman Women Dis Sex-Laden Rap Videos," *Atlanta Journal-Constitution* (April 21, 2004), 1A.
32. Vikki Conwell, "Spelman Rap Protest Derails Charity Event," *Atlanta Journal Constitution* (April 1, 2004).
33. William Jelani Cobb, "Past Imperfect: The Hoodrat Theory," *Africana.com* (April 26, 2004).
34. Kevin Johnson, "Protest Over Nelly Video Pits Raunch Vs. Public Service," *St. Louis Post-Dispatch* (April 18, 2004), F8.
35. Richard L. Elderidge, "Spelman vs. Nelly Dispute Goes National," *Atlanta Journal-Constitution* (April 8, 2004), 2F.
36. Martin Edlund, "Hip-Hop's Crossover to the Adult Aisle," *New York Times* (March 7, 2004), Section 2, page 1.
37. Quoted in Edlund, Section 2, page 1.
38. Quoted in Nekesa Mumbi Moody, "BET Gets Dirty After Dark," *Toronto Star* (April 11, 2004), D05.
39. Joan Morgan, "Sex, Lies and Videos," *Essence Magazine* (June 2002), 124.
40. Cobb.
41. Quoted in Kristen Wyatt, "Black College Women, Sick of Shakin' It, Take Aim at Rappers," *Associated Press* (April 23, 2004).
42. Jayna Brown, "Commentary: Resurgence of the Pimp in the Hip-Hop Culture," *National Public Radio* (October 8, 2003).
43. Moya Bailey, "Dilemma," *Wiretapmag.org* (May 21, 2004).
44. Patricia Hill-Collins, *Black Sexual Politics: African Americans, Gender, and the New Racism* (New York: Routledge, 2004), 29.

45. Hill-Collins, *Black Sexual Politics*, 51.

46. See Jeffrey Melnick, *A Right to Sing the Blues: African-Americans, Jews and American Popular Song* (Cambridge, MA: Harvard University Press, 1999); Eric Lott, *Love and Theft: Blackface Minstrelsy and the American Working Class* (New York: Oxford University Press, 1995).

47. Kevin Powell, "Notes of a Hip-Hop Head," in *Who Shot Ya?: Three Decades of Hiphop Photography*, ed. Kevin Powell (New York: Amistad, 2002), xii.

48. Gwendolyn Pough, Check It While I Wreck: Black Womanhood, Hip-Hop Culture and the Public Sphere (Boston: Northeastern University Press, 2004), 71.

49. Daphne Brooks, "It's Not Right But It's Okay: Black Women's R&B and the House that Terry McMillan Built," SOULS, Vol. 5, No. 1 (March 2003), 32–45.

50. See discussion of Sarah Jones's "Your Revolution," in my book Songs in the Key of Black Life: A Rhythm and Blues Nation (New York: Routledge, 2002).

51. Quoted in Farrell, 27.

52. Bailey, Wiretapmag.org.

53. Quoted in Farrell, 27.

Index

Black aesthetic, 55
Black American Literature Forum, 36
Black Arts Movement, 133
Black Entertainment Television (BET), 2,
    27, 89, 123, 142
Black feminism issues, 153–155
Black feminist fatherhood, 99–125,
    156–157
*Black Feminist Thought: Knowledge,
    Consciousness, and the Politics of
    Empowerment*, 46, 48, 55
Black Gay Man, 27
Black gay men
    DL identities and gay marriage, 79–93
    introduction, 67–79
    mythical notion of, 155–156
    remembering Sakia Gunn, 93–97
Black identity, 28. *see also* Black
    masculinity, crisis of
Black inferiority, 15
*Black Macho and the Myth of the
    Superwoman*, 35–39
*Black Male: Representations of
    Masculinity in Contemporary
    American Art*, 14
Black male feminist
    birth of, 42–53
    heroes and, 53–65
    introduction, 31–42
    sexism and, 127–149
Black male privilege, understanding,
    152–153
A Black Man's Guide to the Black Woman,
    58
Black masculinity, crisis of
    afterword, 151–159
    being a black male in America today,
    16–30, 159
    hip-hop culture versus the Talented
    Tenth, 3–16
    introduction, 1–3
Black Nation, 40
Black Nationalism, 3, 15, 21–22, 37
Black on Both Sides, 127
Black patriarchy, 9, 13, 20, 21, 40
Black Power movement, 22, 68
The Black Scholar, 41
*Black Sexual Politics: African Americans,
    Gender, and the New Racism*, 144
Black Solidarity Day, 67, 73–77

The Black Woman, 41
Black women issues, 153–155
Bonds, Barry, 110
Boorstein, Karen, 39
Boston Globe, 6
*The Boundaries of Blackness: AIDs and
    the Breakdown of Black Politics*, 71, 81
Boycott (film), 29
Brooks, Daphne, 115, 147
Brott, Armin A., 108, 110, 114, 117
Brown, Dee, 7
Brown, Jayna, 143
Brown, Joseph H., 15
Brown, Mark, 14
Brown, Tony, 34, 35
Brown, Sylvester, Jr., 137
Bryant, Kobe, 129
Buffalo News, 5
Bush, George H., 43, 132
Busia, Abena, 49
Butts, Calvin O., 10–11, 87, 88

C

Cannon, Nick, 124
Carbado, Devon, 43, 95
Carmichael, Stokely, 23, 34
Carter, John, 11
Catholic University, 35
Cavanah, Todd, 120
Cedric the Entertainer, 12–13
Center for Disease Control and
    Prevention (CDC), 81, 85
Chang, David, 15
*Check It While I Wreck It: Black
    Womanhood, Hip-Hop Culture,
    and the Public Sphere*, 147
Cheetah Girls, 119
Chenault, Kenneth, 2
Childcare activities, 102
Children's Place, 108
Chinzera, Ayoka, 59
The Chocolate Factory, 27, 120–122
Christian, Barbara, 44
Church of God in Christ (COGIC), 89
Cinderella, 119
Civil Rights Act of 1964, 25
Clark, Leroy, 34, 35
Clark Atlanta University, 143
Clarke, Cheryl, 27